Information Science and Knowledge Management, Vol. 13

Editor-in-Chief

J. Mackenzie Owen

T0181496

Noriko Hara

Communities of Practice

Fostering Peer-to-Peer Learning and
Informal Knowledge Sharing in the
Work Place

 Springer

Noriko Hara, Ph.D.
Indiana University, Bloomington
School of Library & Information Science (SLIS)
1320 East 10th St.
Bloomington IN 47405-3907
USA
nhara@indiana.edu

ISBN: 978-3-642-09910-6   e-ISBN: 978-3-540-85424-1
DOI: 10.1007

Cover design: SPi Publishing Services

Printed on acid-free paper

9 8 7 6 5 4 3 2 1

springer.com

Dedicated to Rob Kling

Acknowledgements

This book would not have existed without initial encouragement from Dr. Elisabeth Davenport. She is the one who introduced me to the Information Science and Knowledge Management series in Springer. I am also thankful to Stefan Goeller at Springer for his assistance in putting this book into a publishable form and for guiding me through my first book-writing experience. Tom Schwen provided great assistance in finding a research site in addition to developing the first manuscript on which this book is based. Khe Hew deserves recognition for the work he did in conducting the data analysis of online messages and for providing critical insights into the discussions presented in Chapter 6. Sharon Stoerger provided important editorial assistance and made time for a careful reading of the final version of the manuscript. I would also like to thank Lijiang Guo, Curt Bonk, Sam Guskin, and study participants. Finally, I would like to thank my husband who diligently edited early drafts and numerous re-writes every night after work. He was my editor, critic, and supporter.

Contents

Contents

Chapter 1
Introduction

1.1 Introduction

Each year corporations spend millions of dollars training and educating their employees. On average, these corporations spend approximately one thousand dollars per employee each year.[1] As businesses struggle to stay on the cutting-edge and to keep their employees educated and up-to-speed with professional trends as well as ever-changing information needs, it is easy to see why corporations are investing more time and money than ever in their efforts to support their employees' professional development.

During the Industrial Age, companies strove to control natural resources. The more resources they controlled, the greater their competitive edge in the marketplace. Senge (1993) refers to this kind of organization as resource-based. In the Information Age, companies must create, disseminate, and effectively use knowledge within their organization in order to maintain their market share. Senge describes this kind of organization as knowledge-based. Given that knowledge-based organizations will continue to be a driving force behind the economy, it is imperative that corporations support the knowledge and information needs of their workers.

In the past, professional development has been discussed within the context of traditional learning;[2] however, traditional learning methods have been criticized for focusing on transmission of explicit knowledge (i.e., they are removed from the context in which knowledge learned is to be practically applied) (Brown, Collins, & Duguid, 1989; Brown & Duguid, 1991; Robey, Khoo, & Powers, 2000). As a result, administrators often fail to see the tangible impact, financial or otherwise, of traditional learning methods on their business because of the difficulties inherent in applying knowledge learned in a traditional classroom setting to the work environment (Smith, 2003).

---

[1] According to the American Society for Training & Development's (ASTD) *2005 State of the Industry Report*, approximately $955 was spent on each employee in 2004, up from $820 in 2003.

[2] See e.g., Freeman & Aspray (1999), for an examination of factors involved in educating an IT workforce.

It is fortuitous then that educators have shifted their focus from an examination of how individuals learn to the impact of the environmental context on individual learners. Current research supports the assertion that, to be truly useful to an organization, learning must take place within an organizational context (Brown & Duguid, 1991; Lave & Wenger, 1991; Wenger, 1998). Consequently, a shift from traditional, codified training methods to a system of learning founded on the establishment of effective learning environments is imperative (Granger, Morbey, Lotherington, Owston, & Wideman, 2002). To help foster the design of such a system, this book calls attention to the importance of informal learning in the training of professionals.

In contrast to traditional knowledge transfer, corporate learning should emphasize the sharing of knowledge by capturing experiences, reusing them, creating new knowledge, and recognizing and solving workplace problems in a process-oriented, collaborative manner (Collins & Margaryan, 2004). Such learning can best be supported via the cultivation of communities of practice.

1.1.1 ICT Use to Support Learning

Since the 1990s, the development of various Information and Communication Technology (ICT) applications has enabled professionals to share ideas and information quickly and effectively. These ICTs include e-mail mailing lists, wikis, electronic bulletin boards, intranets, blogs, and new forms of groupware, such as web-conferencing systems. In educational communities, such systems are classified as e-learning or virtual learning environments, whereas in corporate settings they are often referred to as knowledge management systems.

Administrators of organizations, businesses, and professional associations are increasingly examining the potential of online communication networks that empower members with the ability to share knowledge and engage in ongoing workplace learning and professional development within an organizational context (Davenport & Prusak, 1998; Gray, 2004; Plaskoff, 2003). One important step forward in the study of knowledge sharing and professional development is the aforementioned notion of employing communities of practice, which has gained significant ground in recent years (Cox, 2005; Hung, Tan, Hedberg, & Koh, 2005; Smith, 2003), particularly in the corporate world (Ruhleder, Jordan, & Elmes, 1996; Wenger, McDermott, & Snyder, 2002; Wenger & Snyder, 2000).

1.1.2 Communities of Practice

Use of the term "community of practice" (Lave & Wenger, 1991) provides us with a lens by which we can focus our understanding of informal *collaborative* learning that occurs outside formal classrooms and training environments. The concept of communities of practice was developed by Lave and Wenger, but because the definition of the term "communities of practice" varies from scholar to scholar (Cox, 2005), it is important to establish a precise definition: Communities of practice are collaborative, informal networks that support professional practitioners in their efforts to develop shared understandings and engage in work-relevant knowledge building.

A key component in our understanding of this concept is that a community of practice develops around a certain activity/profession, such as legal practice, medical practice, collaborative efforts of information technology professionals, librarianship, or teaching and instruction. In fact, a shared professional identity is the glue that binds the members of a community together (Wenger, 1998). It is the value system that helps to attract new members to a community and is often a crucial factor in their decision to commit. In past discussions of communities of practice, considerable attention has been paid to the role of informal learning (Johnson, 2001). This is because communities of practice provide environments for fostering informal learning; yet, relatively little attention has been paid to the process of identity formation. This is true especially in the business, information, and computer science fields where communities of practice are often considered an essential component of knowledge management strategies (e.g., Wenger et al., 2002; Wenger & Snyder, 2000).

Although the term "communities of practice" embodies the seemingly romantic image of individuals sharing knowledge with others, such sharing requires complex coordination. If we consider knowledge a resource held in common by an organization, individual workers are often faced with the question of whether or not, to what extent, and under what circumstances should they use, share, and ideally, contribute to this collective resource.

My interest in the concept of communities of practice is rooted in my experience as an instructional designer in a corporate university. After watching and talking with internal clients, I came to the realization that they seemed to be learning more while working with colleagues and using work-relevant skills and knowledge in context than they were when simply sitting in training courses. I was also fortunate to informally observe a group of engineers who had formed a community of practice after taking a less-than-effective training course. At that time, I had not yet been acquainted with the concepts of organizational learning and communities of practice; however, after I returned to graduate school, this topic became one of my major research interest areas.

At present, the concept of communities of practice has attracted considerable interest. Many organizations have attempted to "create" communities of practice within their organizations' knowledge management practice. However, there is debate about whether we can simply create a community of practice. Originally, Lave and Wenger argued that communities of practice emerged, and that they were not something that could be artificially created (Lave & Wenger, 1991; Wenger, 1998). As the concept grew in popularity, some authors began to advocate for the intentional design of communities of practice, especially in electronic environments. Soon thereafter, Wenger et al. (2002) published *Cultivating Communities of Practice*, in which he and his co-authors argued that while communities of practice cannot be "created" per se, communities of practice could be nurtured or cultivated. In doing so, Wenger moved away from a strict view of naturally emerging communities of practice to a view somewhat more in accord with writers advocating for the artificial creation of communities of practice.

In their book, Wenger et al. identified seven actions that could be taken in order to cultivate communities of practice: (1) a community should be designed so that it can evolve naturally; (2) opportunities for the establishment of an open dialogue between inside and outside perspectives should be established; (3) a community should allow for different levels of participation; (4) room for development of both public and private community spaces should be accommodated; (5) the focus of the community should be on the value of the community; (6) a combination of familiarity and excitement should be cultivated; (7) the community should establish a regular rhythm for the community. However, it should be emphasized that this description of traits is not intended as a guide for the creation of a community of practice from scratch. A community of practice is cultivated; it is not imposed upon an existing system.

Similarly, Plaskoff (2003) has suggested a means for fostering communities of practice based on his own experience in a large pharmaceutical company. He notes three concepts that must exist for the successful cultivation of a community of practice within an organization: believing, behaving, and belonging. Believing refers to the idea that members need to believe in the intrinsic value of a community. Behaving indicates that members develop and follow norms of a community. Belonging means that members nurture a sense of belonging within a community. In a personal conversation, Plaskoff mentioned that when he recruited new members of a community of practice, he began by asking questions of the members: What makes a community? Why do you *belong* to a certain community, e.g., a church and/or neighborhood? It was his hope that these types of questions would cause members to consider the three concepts mentioned above.

Several case studies (Schwen & Hara, 2004) indicate the problematic and unsustainable nature of designing communities of practice in a vacuum. Contu and Willmott (2003) have criticized the current trend of "operationalizing" communities of practice. It would seem that one cannot simply impose the concept of communities of practice on an existing professional organization, especially via the mere imposition of online communication tools, and expect a successful community of practice to emerge. Indeed, despite the enthusiasm of some scholars (e.g., Hildreth, 2004; Hung et al., 2005; Schlager, Fusco, & Schank, 1998), online communities of practice have a marked tendency to be hit or miss.

As one could expect, there are some cases of successful online communities of practice. For example, Gray (2004) describes how an online community among the coordinators of the Alberta Community Adult Learning Councils possesses the characteristics of face-to-face communities of practice. Gray highlights peripheral learning opportunities for newcomers, identity support, and the pivotal role a moderator plays in sustaining such a community. *Tapped In* is another widely known successful example of an online community of practice. It is designed to support the professional development of K-12 teachers and has grown from 1,000 members in 1997 to 11,000 in 2001 (Gray & Tatar, 2004).

While there have not been many critical empirical studies of online communities of practice, Kling and Courtright (2004) did analyze one not-quite-successful online community of practice. They identified two primary reasons for this: it was not designed to support the actual practice of the profession, and inadequate attention was paid to the way in which participants needed to develop trust in order to fruitfully share personal practice and knowledge. Schwen and Hara (2004) have cautioned that ICTs are not necessarily advantageous when attempting to nurture communities of practice, and their reviews of the literature show that online communities of practice generally should not be artificially designed. While serious interest in the concept exists, our understanding of the factors that lead to the emergence of successful (or unsuccessful) communities of practice is insufficient. What is needed is to understand more about existing communities of practice and the roles that ICTs play in the support of these communities.

1.2 The Fieldwork

Perhaps the study of communities of practice can take a cue from the field of ethnography. Ethnographers have a longstanding tradition of studying occupational communities (Orr, 1990; Van Maanen & Barley, 1984). As Heath (1981) states, "the goal of ethnography is to describe the ways of living of a social group, usually one in which there is in-group recognition by the members that they indeed must live and work together to retain group identity" (p. 105). Corporate ethnography (e.g., Orr, 1990), sometimes referred to as organizational folklore (Jones, 1991), is one area in which a concept similar to communities of practice is discussed. The focus of this field is on culture in informal or "non-canonical" (Brown & Duguid, 1991) forms of organization. Jones (1988) cites the criticisms of traditionally popular quantitative research in organizational studies and asserts that ethnography is a suitable method to study symbols, myths, and stories in organizations, and to capture the richness of the interaction among members in organizations. Smart (1998) also states that:

> Interpretive ethnography, with its method of "reading" a community's discourse, or system of symbolic forms, offers a researcher a unique way of examining and producing an account of the intellectual collaboration that allows a professional organization to generate and apply specialized written knowledge. (p. 114)

In addition, "articulation work" is a useful notion, which describes "the continuous efforts required in order to bring together discontinuous elements—of organizations, of professional practices, of technologies—into working configurations" (Suchman, 1996, p. 407).

The methodology of corporate ethnographies with attention to articulation work may provide insight for studies of communities of practice. Most organizational theorists focus on the top-down nature of organizational phenomena, whereas ethnographers focus on lower-level employees (Jones, 1991). These two approaches of research should complement each other.

In the present study, my aim was to develop a cohesive understanding of shared knowledge building in communities of practice and the role of ICTs that is informed by an ethnographical perspective.

1.3 The Plan of this Book

As Brown and Duguid (1991) assert, significant learning and innovation arise via informal communities of practice developed in the workplace. This book will examine how people share and construct knowledge in an organization using information technologies such as groupware, e-mail, and online forums, which foster organizational learning, and will seek to discover how ideas are generated, how critical information is disseminated, and how cooperative action arises within organizations. Specifically, it will focus on the important role communities of practice play in the creation and dissemination of pertinent knowledge primarily in two Public Defender's Offices.

In the following chapters, Chapter 2 will expand the key concepts of communities of practice, situated cognition, knowledge sharing and organizational learning, and information communication technologies that appear in the existing literature. Chapter 3 will provide an ethnographic account of a community of practice in a Public Defender's Office in Square County, consisting of excerpts from observation vignettes, interviews, and document review data as well as interpretation and discussion of the data. Chapter 4 will discuss six themes emerged from the ethnographic study presented in Chapter 3. Chapter 5 will provide another ethnographic account of communities of practice in a Public Defender's Office in Circle County. The role of ICTs in supporting public defenders' practices is examined within the communities of practice. Chapter 6 will introduce online communities of practice that are beyond organizational boundaries. Finally, Chapter 7 will discuss cross-case analyses, the summary of the study, naturalistic generalization, future research opportunities, and implications of these studies.

Chapter 2
Theoretical Foundation

2.1 Introduction

Our understanding of "communities of practice" originates within the theoretical framework of situated cognition, which itself is rooted in socio-cultural theory (Vygotsky, 1978) and criticism of mainstream educational psychology (i.e., the tendency of behaviorists to separate learning and cognition from the context in which learning takes place) (Brown, Collins, & Duguid, 1989). By expanding the theoretical framework of situated cognition, the term "communities of practice" is able to describe systematic group behaviors exhibited when learning takes place *in situ*.

Our understanding of communities of practice is sometimes muddled because it is often mentioned in connection with other related topics. It is important to the present discussion that we understand how the concept of a community of practice has evolved over time within the context of other scholarship. For example, the concept of communities of practice has been related to organizational learning although Lave and Wenger (1991), the originators of the term, focused on apprenticeship not organizational learning. Brown and Duguid (1991) were actually the first to explicitly point out the connection between the two concepts, and from that time forward, there has been a tendency to consider these two concepts as related. In addition to organizational learning, communities of practice foster knowledge sharing, and the concept is also invoked in discussions of knowledge management. Furthermore, many authors now contend that information technologies can help communities of practice advance and expand beyond physical boundaries (e.g., Gray, 2004; Hung & Chen, 2001; Pan & Leidner, 2003; Sharp, 1997), including Wenger (2001) himself.

In this chapter, I will clarify the relationship of communities of practice to those other concepts by providing a preliminary literature review of: (1) situated cognition, (2) organizational learning, (3) communities of practice, (4) knowledge management, and (5) information technologies, as they relate to communities of practice. In doing so, I will attempt to elucidate the theoretical roots of communities of practice, as well as review recent discussions of communities of practice.

N. Hara, *Communities of Practice: Fostering Peer-to-Peer Learning and Informal Knowledge Sharing in the Work Place*, Information Science and Knowledge Management 13,
© Springer-Verlag Berlin Heidelberg 2009

2.2 Research in Cognate Areas Relevant to the Topic

2.2.1 Situated Cognition

Situated cognition as a theoretical framework originated primarily in reaction to the concerns educators had in identifying an optimal classroom learning environment for K-12 children. Brown et al. (1989), along with Lave (1988), advocated learning via participation and situational immersion rather than sitting through traditional lectures, which emphasizes learning by rote and repetition. Unlike Lave (1988) who studied how ordinary folks are able to perform math problems in real-life situations (e.g., how to add and subtract numbers when buying goods at a grocery store or when participating in a Weight Watchers program), Brown et al. (1989) emphasized situated cognition as a means of facilitating formal learning *in the classroom* in order to make "structured" learning more meaningful. As stated previously, our understanding of situated cognition has its origin in the theoretical framework of Vygotsky's socio-cultural theory (1978). Vygotsky also emphasized the importance of environment in establishing positive, dynamic learning processes for children. Plaskoff (2003) himself would later remark that "the apprenticeship model from which Lave and Wenger derive the concept of CoPs demonstrates these Vygoskian principles in action" (p. 164).

Similarly, George, Iacono, and Kling (1995) have stated that "learning is a *group-level* phenomenon which is an essential part of daily work practices" (p. 2, emphasis mine). In their study, they compare the occupational status of the managerial and clerical members of a work group and the manner in which these two types of workers exhibited different styles of implementing computer systems. At the heart of their study is an investigation of the factors that affect learning in context. To this end, they identified three characteristics of the work group environment that influenced learning in context:

1. The degree of value and/or recognition by management placed upon the various work roles in the clerical and professional workers;
2. The degree of participation in legitimate peripheral learning permitted under various working conditions; and
3. The presence of opportunities for participation in unofficial communities of practice (e.g., grassroots computing implementations).

George et al. also affirmed the importance of positive, participatory learning environments including those relevant to working conditions and the noncanonical practices of co-workers. One of their core findings was identification of the correlation between the status of work groups and the strategy of technology implementation; they concluded that "professional work groups are associated with grass roots implementations, while clerical groups are associated with top down implementations, and mixed occupation work groups are squarely in the middle" (p. 21). In short, George et al. recognized an important issue for future research: understanding the links between learning and performance.

Undoubtedly, learning occurs within social contexts (Brown & Duguid, 2000; Resnick, Levine, & Teasley, 1991; Ruhleder, Jordan, & Elmes, 1996; Vygotsky, 1978; Wenger, 1996, 1998). Lave and Wenger (1991) have pointed out the importance of "shifting the analytic focus from the individual as learner to learning as participation in the social world, and from the concept of cognitive process to the more-encompassing view of social practice" (p. 43). In addition, George et al. (1995) have noted the correlation between learning and performance. Therefore, wherever situated cognition occurs in the workplace, it is only natural that one will find the seeds of a potentially robust community of practice.

2.2.2 Organizational Learning

Herbert A. Simon first discussed the idea of organizational learning conceptually in 1953 (Kuchinke, 1995); however, Cyert and March (1963) were the first to define learning "as a fundamental organizational process" (Cohen & Lee, 1991). After the publication of Cyert and March's article in 1963, the term "organizational learning" became moderately popular in the field of management science and organizational studies. When Senge (1990) revisited the concept and coined the term "learning organization," management consultants became interested (Cohen & Sproull, 1996). Basically, organizational learning refers to the idea that organizations, as a whole, can learn from previous experiences.

Recently, two forms of organizational learning have been identified in the literature, namely "single-loop" and "double-loop" learning (Argyris, 1991). Single-loop organizational learning is sometimes referred to as "adaptive learning" (Senge, 1990), i.e., learning via adaptation to routine. Double-loop organizational learning, on the other hand, is frequently called "generative learning" (Senge, 1990), that is learning evolves (or is "generated") as a result of reflection. However, this distinction between single-loop and double-loop learning is artificial and simplifies what is actually a rather complicated process. It is oftentimes difficult to determine precisely how learning is taking place on an organizational level. Moreover, the single-double distinction assumes that organizational learning is necessarily positive. As Miller (1996) states, "learning is to be distinguished from decision making. The former increases organizational knowledge, the latter need not" (p. 486).

Within the organizational learning literature,[1] there are two distinctive and identifiable positions. Weick & Westley (1996) differentiate between the way an individual learns in an organizational context and how organizations learn (i.e., via the accumulation of collective experience). The former is referred to as the "cognitive perspective" (Argyris, 1991; Levitt & March, 1988; Simon, 1996) or "acquisition metaphor" (Elkjaer, 2004), and is analogous to Argyris's (1991) description of single-loop and double-loop learning. The latter is referred to as the "cultural perspective" (Blackler, 1995; Cook & Yanow, 1996; Weick & Westley, 1996) or

---

[1] See Easterby-Smith, Antonacopoulou, Simm, and Lyles (2004) for a more detailed historical overview of the literature in organizational learning.

"participation metaphor" (Elkjaer, 2004), and refers to how an organization as a whole learns from previous mistakes. Each perspective focuses on learning; yet the "cognitive perspective" tends to focus on individual psychological factors, whereas the "cultural perspective" focuses on organizational culture.

Argyris (1991) is considered an acolyte of the school of cognitive perspective (Cook & Yanow, 1996). His explanation of learning focuses on individual learning within organizations. Argyris has stated that double-loop learning is a "reflection of how people think" (p. 100). However, when contrasted with the aforementioned "cultural perspective," his argument comes across as being too narrowly focused on individuals.

The "cultural perspective" is closely related to the concept of communities of practice. Cook and Yanow's 1996 paper, which expounded upon the benefits of the cultural perspective, criticized the use of the cognitive perspective to study organizational learning for the three reasons: first, an ambiguous distinction between learning in organizations and learning by organizations is made; second, they argue, organizations do not learn the same way as individuals do; and third, the cognitive perspective tends to focus heavily on behavioral changes and gives minimal attention to issues like cultural identity. Cook and Yanow argued, therefore, that viewing organizational learning from a cultural perspective has advantages because of the particular attention it pays to cultural identity within organizations. They contended that "cultural organizational learning would focus on the *mutual* creation of compatible and shared meanings" (p. 454) and reached the conclusion that organizations, like individuals, can learn.

Along the similar lines, ? (?) proposed an alternative perspective of the study of organizational learning, namely, viewing organizations as cultures, which allowed for more focus on the practices of groups than on the activities of individuals. They also asserted that "conceptualizing organizations as cultures makes it easier to talk about learning" (p. 442). In doing so, Weick and Westley endorsed a position that equates organizational learning to situations in which individuals learn in a social context via their interaction with others. It should be understood that this definition of organizational learning is not the same as that in which the organization itself learns.

Inside any organization viewed within a framework of organizations as cultures, finding a balance between exploration and exploitation is important for organizational learning because, as ? (?) state, "it is evident that either form, taken to its extreme, results in a paralysed organization, unable either to learn or to act" (p. 445). This is similar to the claim that Davenport, Jarvenpaa, and Beers (1996) made in their discussion of knowledge improvement methodology. They noted that improvement methods work better near the middle of the continuum – between a "laissez-faire approach" and a "reengineering approach." Similarly, Weick and Westley concluded that "people learn how to innovate, but they also learn how to reaccomplish their identity amidst a new set of threats" (p. 448).

In discussing innovation and knowledge creation, Nonaka (1991) bridged the gap between individual learning and organizational learning by criticizing Western cultural views of knowledge as "objective information." He stressed that creating new knowledge "depends on tapping the tacit and often highly subjective insights, intuitions, and hunches of individual employees" (p. 97). In order to create an environment in which knowledge shared among small pockets of employees is captured and distributed within an organization, Nonaka developed a framework for knowledge creation in organizations. He described the development of a bridge between individual learning within organizations and learning by organizations through the knowledge conversion process involving the acquisition of tacit knowledge, conversion of tacit knowledge to explicit knowledge, the sharing of explicit knowledge, and then internalization of explicit knowledge. The result is internalization of tacit knowledge by individuals within the organization.

In 1991, Brown and Duguid supported their analysis of the relationship between organizational learning and communities of practice by referring to the example of the Xerox field technicians studied by Orr (1990, 1996). They stated that communities of practice developed among technicians as a result of the necessity of making it possible for people who worked in the same region to learn from each other. Often, this exchange of tacit knowledge took place within the context of storytelling. As illustrated by the technicians in Orr's study and the "skills people" in Zuboff's (1988) earlier study, storytelling is fundamental to fostering knowledge among people because it helps to develop a shared understanding. In addition, it provides situational context and is appealing because of its improvisational nature. Storytelling is also a tool for the conversion of tacit knowledge to explicit knowledge (externalization) á la Nonaka's (1991) model.

Although "cultural perspectives" are vital to understanding organizational learning, to entertain the notion that an organization learns on its own without consideration for the individual is unsound. The distinction between individual learning and organizational learning is of vital importance. Learning, as has been argued, can occur on different levels – the organizational as well as group and individual levels (Bapuji & Crossan 2004). Learning can be an individual experience as well as a social phenomenon. Each individual processes learning acquired in social contexts by him- or herself. This concept, that organizational learning results when a group of individuals learn and participate in organization activities, is, for all practical purposes, analogous to conceptions of communities of practice (Hara, 2000). Elkjaer (2004) has called it a "third way" of organizational learning, emphasizing the need to synthesize both the acquisition and the participatory nature of learning in order to expand current research on organizational learning.

2.2.3 Communities of Practice

Lave and Wenger coined the term "community of practice" in 1991. Their original definition emphasized "legitimate peripheral participation," a form of apprenticeship that allows newcomers to participate at the edge of a community while learning the lingo and developing an intuitive sense of the shared identity of the community. The end result of this process is assimilation into the community (Lave & Wenger,

1991); their focus was on newcomers to an existing community of practice. The following is Lave and Wenger's original definition:

> A community of practice is a set of relations among persons, activity, and world, over time and in relation with other tangential and overlapping communities of practice. A community of practice is an intrinsic condition for the existence of knowledge, not least because it provides the interpretive support necessary for making sense of its heritage. Thus, participation in the cultural practice in which any knowledge exists is an epistemological principle of learning. The social structure of this practice, its power relations, and its condition for legitimacy define possibilities for learning (i.e., legitimate peripheral participation). (p. 98)

More recently, this term has become established in the corporate world (e.g., Brown & Duguid, 2000; Hildreth, 2004; Ruhleder et al., 1996; Wenger et al., 2002; Wenger & Snyder, 2000), and many companies have tried to facilitate the formal creation of communities of practice to improve knowledge sharing within their organizations.

Deviating from the original definition of Lave and Wenger, the definition I use here focuses on fostering opportunities for knowledge sharing in professional CoPs. This approach is similar to that of Orr (1990, 1996) as well as Brown and Duguid (1991) in its focus on the activity in the workplace. Brown and Duguid criticized the paradigm that dominates current training programs (i.e., learning by rote) because training in classrooms separates the act of learning from the act of working. As an alternative, they introduced the concept of "learning-in-working" and pictured learning as a bridge between work and innovation.

Orr's (1996) ethnographic study indicated that work practices are different from what organizations describe officially. To illustrate this argument, the example of a "work-to-rule" strike, a method of striking used by organized labor in France is useful (Scott, 1998). Under a work-to-rule strike, workers perform their work following their (often incomplete) job descriptions exactly. The result is a dysfunctional work place. This behavior highlights how, in reality, most jobs are quite different from their official descriptions. A lack of consideration for the distinction between what workers are told to do and what they actually *need* to do to perform their jobs results in a disconnect in which the training programs provided by organizations and what the employees actually need to improve their job performance are out of synch.

Although Brown and Duguid (1991) use Orr's study to describe the concept of communities of practice, Orr (1990, 1996) himself does not use this term. Indeed, when asked about his study, Orr replied that his original intent in conducting his study of Xerox technicians was not to study a community of practice, but to illustrate technicians' work practices (personal communication, 1998). Thus, Orr (1990) uses the term "community memory" (p. 169) to describe the knowledge sharing process in the community of technicians while simultaneously emphasizing the importance of information exchange within this community. Without using the term "community of practice," Orr describes one.

The particular group of technicians that Orr (1990) studied worked in a culture that encouraged mutual support. For instance, they had a place to "hang out" during their lunch break, and if one of them had a problem, s/he could always ask for help during this time. Because this group of people repaired many of the same types of machines, they benefited from a social setting in which to share solutions as well as seek help with problems. This brings us back to our discussion of storytelling: "There appears to be every incentive to share information and virtually none to keep it private 'because' there is no way to solve a difficult problem and have it known without telling the story" (Orr, 1990, p. 174). Within this social setting, they learned to tell stories by listening to other technicians' stories. Once they learned how to tell stories, they became full members of the community of practice. The technicians told stories for three reasons: (1) practically (and perhaps subconsciously), they shared information in order to work more efficiently; (2) it is easier to remember the "war" stories told by other technicians because the stories are situated within a context; and (3) they wanted to display their competence and make their stories interesting.

> [T]he characteristics of the work are such that the only way for one's work to be known to one's peers is to tell them, and the only way to make it interesting is to have a difficult problem and present it so as to be recognized as such by other competent practitioners. (Orr, 1990, p. 174)

Orr (1990) concluded that the technicians' "community memory is about being a technician, and it helps them to be technicians." (p. 187). One place where workers may share and build community memory is in a community of practice.

Of course, not all scholars have reacted positively to the concept of communities of practice. A handful has discussed negative aspects of communities of practice (Huysman, 2002). Among the few, Henriksson (2000) criticized overwhelming enthusiasm for the concept. She claimed that CoPs may not represent organizational reality and suggested that researchers keep the concept in alignment with organizational cultural research.[2] Huysman (2002) also discussed an example of how a community of practice that developed among IT professionals demonstrated negative impacts on the organization. Furthermore, Fox (2000) has criticized the lack of discussion about individual and/or group abuse of power in the research of communities of practice. However, the concept is still extremely useful for articulating collective knowledge creation within organizations.

The following section discusses five attributes of communities of practice: (1) a group of professional practitioners; (2) development of shared meaning; (3) informal social networks; (4) a supportive culture, and (5) engagement in knowledge building. Each attribute is described in detail below.

2.2.3.1 Group of Professional Practitioners

A community, by definition, involves at least two members. However, Orr (1990, 1996) has pointed out that professionals prefer autonomy. No one can force the members of a CoP to learn together or to share information (Stamps, 1997; Stewart, 1996). Yet, professionals will work in groups. It is essential that professionals share knowledge collectively if a community of practice is to be fostered. Studies have

---

[2] That includes research on organizational learning from the cultural perspective, such as the work by Yanow (2000).

shown that even characteristically autonomous professionals (i.e., technicians [Orr, 1990, 1996], nurses [Hara & Hew, 2007], coordinators for adult learning councils [Gray, 2004], reference service users [Davenport, 2001], and workers in a pharmaceuticals company [Hayes & Walsham, 2001]) have developed successful communities of practice. As mentioned above, the formation of a community of practice may hinge on something as simple as the opportunity to share work stories in a social context.

2.2.3.2 Development of a Shared Meaning

"As people work together, they not only learn from doing, they develop a shared sense of what has to happen to get the job done" (Stamps, 1997). Information exchanged in communities of practice is communicated among members. This most basic social process results in the development of shared meanings (Montovani, 1996). Since each community of practice exists within a specific context (Wenger, 1998), the shared meanings that evolve are situated within this context. In order to communicate effectively, the development of shared meaning and means for the exchange of knowledge are essential (Davenport & Hall, 2002; Krauss & Fussell, 1990; Plaskoff, 2003). While Plaskoff has emphasized the importance of developing a common vocabulary, a common language not only indicates a shared comprehension of explicit knowledge (e.g., meaning of words), but also signifies the existence of tacit knowledge (e.g., metaphors and values).

2.2.3.3 Informal Networks

Schwen and Hara (2004) caution that communities of practice cannot be artificially created or implemented. Communities of practice are difficult to identify and isolate for a study because they exhibit organizational patterns that are not reflected in hierarchal organizational charts. This is because communities of practice are *informal* networks that evolve organically. In this sense, they are akin to the unforced relationships that develop over time between friends and colleagues. Even Wenger (1996) has asserted that "there is no distinction between learning [within communities of practice] and social participation."

One example of how people help each other informally is described in a study conducted by Leitzman (1981). In this study faculty members were interviewed and asked in what situations they would turn to colleagues for help; however, many of those interviewed considered the term "help" too official. Instead they preferred to describe what they were doing as the "sharing of common experiences" (p. 4.36). Leitzman posited that this tendency toward informality might be a mechanism intended to protect one's "teaching reputation in a competitive climate" (p. 4.37) because if a faculty member had officially asked for "help," it may have been construed by others that s/he was not competent to teach.

Likewise Kling and Courtright (2004) address how the issue of trust prevented teachers from actively participating in a community of practice. When discussing challenges within the profession with their colleagues, the teachers felt a need to develop a sense of trust before feeling comfortable enough to be candid when sharing their experiences. In a similar vein, O'Leary, Orlikowski, and Yates (2002), in their historical analysis of Hudson's Bay Company, describe the need for finding a balance between trust and control within the group dynamic.

2.2.3.4 Supportive Culture

Communities of practice help to develop a supportive culture. More importantly, members of communities of practice come to trust each other – at the very least, on a professional level (Davenport & Hall, 2002). For example, in Orlikowski's (1996) seminal study, the supportive culture which existed in the department of customer representatives precipitated the development of a CoP. A specialist in the department commented that attention was not paid to who received credit for what information; but rather, information was shared in order to support the collective assignments of each of the department's co-workers. Although they were not officially in a team, the community established the notion of working as a team. Another specialist in the department provided the following example: sometimes she would see a co-worker struggling to answer an overwhelming number of incoming phone calls and offer to help; or if she saw someone having a problem similar to one that she had previously encountered, she offered suggestions. Such behavior suggests that the culture of this department was cooperative.

2.2.3.5 Engagement in Knowledge Building

Learning is a process of knowledge acquisition and identification of the relationship between facts and ideas. Communities of practice represent systems whereby members acquire and share knowledge collectively. However, it is important to keep in mind that individuals are autonomous learners; they learn for themselves and not necessarily for the benefit of the organization. If the organization benefits at all, it is through the development of less selfish avenues of exchange (i.e., the genesis of communities of practice within the organization).

"[M]uch of what has been written about networks at work has been concerned, in part, with community" (Kling, 1996, p. 426); however, oftentimes managers have paid inadequate attention to importance of informal professional communities because they are usually founded on social networks. Kling states that "communities that are based on people caring about and taking responsibility for the well-being of their members are harder to build" (p.434). In other words, communities of practice are developed via the cultivation of trust and mutual respect – two characteristics that can be easily undone. This observation is consistent with those made by others, such as Stewart (1996) or Stamps (2000). Stamps further assert that "while it's generally agreed that CoPs cannot be commanded by management dictum or jump-started by technology, it is very easy to destroy them by meddling – even when the meddling is a well-intentioned effort to nurture them" (p. 62). As Huysman (2003) argues, management can sometimes inadvertently harm the mechanisms by which communities of practice manage knowledge.

In 2003, Contu and Willmott analyzed the then-current discussion of Lave and Wenger's seminal book, *Situated Learning*, and criticized popular interpretations of communities of practice in that they inadvertently downplay (or overlook altogether) any consideration of the power embedded in the original concept of communities of practice. They pointed out that Lave and Wenger emphasized the historic situational context in which learning occurs. As such, Contu and Willmott's conclusions called for a more holistic view of learning, which incorporates a consideration of history, language, and power in organizations. In addition, Fox (2000) has criticized the lack of focus on the issue of power and has proposed using actor network theory as a theoretical framework for the examination of power within organizations – primarily because actor network theory can provide rigorous structures that will facilitate a clearer understanding of the issue of power.

While consideration must be given to the critiques of Contu and Willmott as well as Fox, these types of discussions indicate the need to explore more areas relevant to the concept of communities of practice in addition to its practical and useful implication to practice.

2.2.4 Knowledge Management

Although the discourse of knowledge management in the popular press peaked in 2002 (Hara & Kling, 2006), the significance of this discussion has not been diminished. We still need to understand what motivates people to share knowledge (Østerlund & Carlile, 2005; Wasko & Faraj, 2005). This section will review briefly how the conceptualization of knowledge has changed, review the literature of knowledge sharing, and discuss the knowledge management literature from the social informatics perspective.

2.2.4.1 Knowledge

Many scholars distinguish between knowledge as object (the objectivist paradigm) and knowledge as process (the constructivist paradigm). Blackler (1995), Lave (1988), and Orlikowski (2002), however, propose that knowledge be analyzed as an active process (knowing), using a *social constructivist* paradigm. Within this paradigm, knowledge (i.e., knowing) is viewed as both an individual and a social process because knowledge is constructed individually and collectively. Lave (1988) and Montovani (1996) have criticized cognitive scientists for failing to place adequate emphasis on the separation between experimental and everyday situations when defining knowledge. For our discussion, knowledge is defined as the process by which a person or a group of people acquire a situated understanding within social context.

2.2.4.2 Knowledge Sharing

Huysman (2002) identifies three potential traps that communities may fall into when sharing knowledge: the management trap, the individual learning trap, and the information and communication technology trap. Further, she states that top-down knowledge management strategies more often than not fail. George et al. (1995) describe a case in which a new IT project was implemented with a top-down strategy and point out the ineffectiveness of this approach. They contrast this with a more effective learning process, a grassroots initiative, in which a group of professionals engaged in informal learning within their community of practice. In Huysman's (2002) view, traditional situations for supporting individual learning, such as conventional instructor-led classes and database searching, are difficult to transform into socially shared processes. Huysman states that some types of tacit knowledge are difficult to share using information technologies (IT). Swan, Robertson, and Newell (2002) raise similar concerns with regard to IT-based knowledge management. To counter this, Huysman and Wulf (2005) propose coupling the concept of communities of practice with that of social capital because social trust is a necessary component for the successful sharing and building of collective goods, i.e., knowledge, among the participants.

It is important to examine why people share knowledge. Wasko and Faraj (2005) find the motivation for individuals to share knowledge on a listserv includes the potential for increasing one's personal reputation, having experiences that they wish to share, and maintaining the central role on the listserv. However, despite expectations, they did not find that commitment to the community or an expectation of reciprocal input motivated individuals to share knowledge. On the other hand, Hew and Hara (2007a) find that both expected and direct reciprocal engagement, commitment to the group, and personal gain are the top three motivators for knowledge sharing in the three listservs they studied. Obviously, further studies are needed to scrutinize what motivates individuals to share knowledge.

2.2.4.3 Knowledge Management from Social Informatics Perspective

Knowledge Management (KM) is a concept that can be applied to a variety of issues and ideas from data mining to the organization of knowledge in systems to philosophical discussions on the nature of knowledge to the development of communities of practice.[3] It is not my intent to discuss each possible application of the KM concept. Rather, I will limit my review of the KM literature to those elements relevant

---

[3] See Prusak (2001), for origins of Knowledge Management.

to the social informatics perspective as first identified by Kling, Rosenbaum, and Sawyer (2005): (1) the use of ICTs leads to multiple and sometimes paradoxical effects; (2) the use of ICTs shapes thoughts and actions in ways that benefit some groups more than others; (3) the differential effects of the design, implementation, and uses of ICTs often have moral and ethical consequences; (4) the design, implementation, and uses of ICTs have reciprocal relationships within the larger social milieu; and (5) ICTs are conceptualized differently by diverse social groups.

The Use of ICTs Leads to Multiple and Sometimes Paradoxical Effects

Within the context of learning, organizing, and belonging, Chae and Bloodgood (2004) have identified paradoxes relevant to knowledge management. One also notes a learning paradox when examining the comparative utility of purposeful and situated learning. Learning can be arranged purposefully by management through formal training or by using KM systems. On the other hand, unintentional and natural learning, so-called "situated learning" (Lave & Wenger, 1991), occurs in work places. The paradox lies in the fact that, while situated learning is difficult to manage, it is often much more effective than purposeful learning (e.g., Hara & Schwen, (2006).

Chae and Bloodgood (2004) also identify a paradox within formal and informal structures implemented in order to support KM activities. Formal structures include KM systems and processes that capture, restore, and distribute job-related knowledge accumulated by employees within organizations. Alternatively, informal structures include ad hoc knowledge sharing opportunities. An especially relevant example of an informal structure is a community of practice (Wenger, 1998) in which formal structures may not be sustainable (Schwen & Hara, 2004). For instance, while a community of practice needs to emerge naturally with bottom-up initiatives, it can be cultivated by a formal structure (Wenger et al., 2002). In other words, managers should not "create" a community of practice, but they should recognize the value of communities of practice and work to provide a nourishing environment by providing necessary resources.

The Use of ICTs Shapes Thoughts and Actions in Ways that Benefit Some Groups More than Others

The KM literature often claims that KM is beneficial for organizations as a whole; further, it makes the assumption that KM will specifically benefit individual employees (Alter, 2006; Hara & Kling, 2006). As the old adage goes, knowledge is power. Those with it succeed; those without it fail.[4]

---

[4] That is, unless of course, the have-nots possess an overwhelming share of brute force. Of course, we might then consider another idiom, namely that violence is the refuge of the powerless (i.e., the knowledge-less).

Ekbia and Hara (2005) have commented upon the difficulty inherent in situations known as *social dilemmas* – namely, those interactions where individuals act rationally (e.g., in their efforts to maximize individual gain) but in which their rational acts lead to collective irrationality (c.f., Cabrera & Cabrera, 2002; Kollock, 1992). Thus, knowledge sharing can be understood as a special type of social dilemma (Cabrera & Cabrera, 2002; Connolly, Thorn, & Heminger, 1992). For example, free-riders sometimes become winners, whereas contributors who share their knowledge may become losers – a fact likely attributable to a lack of assertiveness and propriety.

The Differential Effects of the Design, Implementation, and Uses of ICTs Often have Moral and Ethical Consequences

Introducing KM initiatives within organizations frequently results in moral and ethical challenges.[5] Recently, Alter (2006) identified three attributes of the "dark side" of KM: distortion, suppression, and misappropriation. Distortion of knowledge refers to the manipulation of knowledge in order to shape it to support specific, biased perspectives. For example, Alter cites biased medical studies sponsored by pharmaceutical companies. Suppression of knowledge is a process in which not all knowledge is shared, thus making it difficult to gain a holistic understanding of an issue and to see the implications of a cause of action; actions of the Chinese government present pertinent examples, such as negotiating with Google to ban anti-government websites or websites containing information on Falun Gong, Tibet's independence, and the Tiananmen Square massacre (e.g., Sabbagh, 2006). Misappropriation of knowledge refers to theft, the inappropriate sale of knowledge, or misrepresentation of facts. An example would be the misappropriation of millions of Americans' personal information by identity thieves who hack into large data storage companies (Dash, 2005).

Similarly, Bryant (2006) identified both the light and dark sides of KM. Of note, he expressed concern that the dark side of KM has the potential to dominate KM's positive aspects. Bryant argues that KM is doing more harm to workers by conceptualizing knowledge as a commodity and jeopardizing the job security of workers who contribute to KM systems.

Another ethical consideration is the question of who owns knowledge. Baskerville and Dulipovici (2006) cite the *DSC Communications, Inc. v. Evan Brown* lawsuit. The court ruled that the company who employed Evan Brown owned the ideas he generated. This verdict seems to suggest that "companies may own employee thoughts" (Baskerville & Dulipovici, 2006, p. 2). It will be interesting to see if this case serves as a precedent for future cases.

---

[5] The 39th Hawaii International Conference on System Sciences mini-track on the Ethics of KM explicitly solicited articles addressing ethics, politics, and the dark side of KM.

The Design, Implementation and Uses of ICTs have Reciprocal Relationships
within the Larger Social Milieu

When organizations implement ICTs, they need to consider the context in which
the KM system is being implemented. Bryant (2006) questions the feasibility of
convincing employees of U.S. companies to share knowledge because of widespread
concern about job security. The employee knowledge sharing trend was precipitated
by Nonaka's 1995 book *The Knowledge Creating Company*. But as Bryant points
out, the book examines knowledge sharing practices in Japanese companies in the
mid-1980s and early 1990s, a time during which when employees enjoyed lifetime
employment and job security. Currently, employees in U.S. companies should be
concerned about their job security (Aeppel, 2002; Baskerville & Dulipovici, 2006).
As such, context must be considered when analyzing the relative success of ICT
implementation.

Seminal articles examining the importance of context in KM system success include Orlikowski's studies (1993, 1996) analyzing the use of Lotus Notes in two
organizations. She attributed dissimilar ICT use levels to differences in the culture
of the organizations (e.g., competitive vs. supportive) and the ability of existing
workflows to accommodate the KM system. More recently, a study of ten public
and private organizations in South Korea (Kim & Lee, 2005) found that specific
contexts, including the presence or absence of social networks, performance-based
reward systems, and/or ICT usage by employees, had a significant impact on knowledge sharing.

In addition, different KM practices within and outside of organizational boundaries have been observed. In a study of knowledge sharing within a longstanding online community of practice (Hara & Hew, 2007), critical care and advanced practice
nurses reported that knowledge sharing was more likely to occur with individuals
outside of a person's own organization because of a lack of concern about promotion
and reward issues. This study's findings offer a meaningful contrast to earlier studies
that examined knowledge sharing practices within organizations where employees
were more reluctant to share their expertise.

ICTs are Conceptualized Differently by Diverse Social Groups

As mentioned earlier, various groups have diverse ways of conceptualizing the same
ICT. The literature on KM, for instance, has a tendency to report the perspectives
of managers and technological designers/implementers to the unfortunate exclusion
of the perspectives of local participating groups (i.e., actual workers who engage in
KM practices). Schultze and Leidner (2002) systematically examined the characteristics of KM research published in six international information systems journals
between 1990 and 2000. Only 28% of the studies (21 out of 75) examined KM
from the perspective of local participating groups as opposed to 72% of the studies
conducted from "elite" perspectives (i.e., those of managers and researchers). It is
vital to acknowledge that floor workers have different perspectives about KM – and
that some of these are not as enthusiastic as their managers (e.g., Aeppel, 2002).

Barth (2000) highlights a dysfunctional mismatch of technological frames between employees and management. As part of performance reviews, IBM employees were asked to contribute their project experience to a company-wide KM system. However, many employees did not submit their contributions until the very last month preceding the reviews. The behavior can be understood in light of the additional burden of the activity, which would have taken away from the time employees would normally have had to spend on job-related tasks.

2.2.5 Information and Communication Technologies

To further deepen understanding of ICT use, Lamb and Kling (2003) examine the traditional conceptualization of users by researchers studying Human-Computer Interaction (HCI) and Computer-Supported Cooperative Work (CSCW). They state that HCI and CSCW researchers tend to focus excessively on individual cognitive tasks and view "users" as isolated individuals, not as individuals within a social context.[6] As an alternative to the term "user," Lamb and Kling propose using the term "interactor." Interactors use information and communication technologies in social contexts. The present study incorporates Lamb and Kling's concept of interactor when the uses of information technologies are discussed.

Similarly, Ruhleder et al. (1996) take the position that "learning and problem-solving are situated, collective activities, and that organizational learning is best understood as a phenomenon that is located in the formal and informal social grouping that makes up an organization" (p. 2). In order to support an organization that learns,

> the work pace and style also required a new set of technologies that would support a '24 × 7' flexible work environment, that would provide information access regardless of time or place, and that would allow for meaningful organization of mission-critical information. (Ruhleder et al., 1996, p. 4)

Information Technology (IT) in such an organization must be flexible, and employees should be able to adapt technologies to fit local needs. For example, in the organization Ruhleder et al. studied, a Notes database called Work Manager was found to be unsuited to supporting employee activities. As a result, a local Notes expert was brought in to "tailor" the database to employee needs. In this organization, managers and IT staff considered how technology fit into people's work practice, not how people fit into technology. This is a sound socio-technical perspective (Ciborra, 1993).

Much research examines the role of technology in supporting work activity (e.g. Galegher, Kraut & Egido, 1990). In particular, interest in examining how ICTs can support distributed communities of practice has grown with the advent of the Internet (Wenger, 2001).[7]

---

[6] This criticism parallels the discussion of knowledge by Lave (1988).

[7] Wenger discusses a series of commercial software products available for the support of so-called online communities of practice such as Communispace (a product designed for enabling community building activities on the web), WebBoard for online discussions, and wiki for collaborative knowledge repositories.

However, despite the enthusiasm of some scholars (e.g., Schlager, Fusco, & Schank, 1998, 2002), online communities of practice have a tendency to be hit or miss – some are successful and some are not. *INDISCHOOL* is one example of a successful online community of practice. It is designed to support the professional development of K-12 teachers. As of December 2005, over 87,000 teachers had become members of *INDISCHOOL*, which represents approximately 54% of the elementary school teachers in Korea (Hur & Hara, 2007).

On the whole, past studies have not expanded on the existing framework of communities of practice, which are based on legitimate peripheral participation (Lave & Wenger, 1991), situated cognition, and identity formation (Wenger, 1998). There exists a need to develop a theoretical framework that incorporates online communities of practice.

Perhaps the best known framework used to study online knowledge sharing is Cyber Ba, literally "cyber place" (Nonaka & Konno, 1998). Basically, Cyber Ba provides an environment for distributing explicit knowledge to others. However, this model does not address the issues of collective learning and identity formation, both of which are core components of the communities of practice concept. More recently, Dubé, Bourhis, and Jacob (2006) have developed a typology of online communities of practice with four dimensions: demographics, organizational context, members, and technological environments. However, their typology was developed independent of face-to-face communities of practice.

When considering online communities of practice, it is apparent that there is a need to investigate how they differ from face-to-face communities of practice. Only by identifying the differences (and similarities) of online and face-to-face communities of practice can we make informed decisions about the application of the concept to online communities.

2.3 Summary of What is Known and Unknown

Overall, research into communities of practice lacks somewhat a substantial body of empirical evidence from which researchers may draw meaningful conclusions (Hara & Kling, 2002); the same holds true for online communities of practice (Dubé et al., 2006; Johnson, 2001).

The debate relevant to the design of communities of practice is worth summarizing. Wenger (1998) once claimed that "learning cannot be designed" (p. 225 & 229). Basically, a worker's motivation for learning is an important precondition and cannot be designed. However, Wenger, like Brown and Duguid (1991), believes that learning can be facilitated. "The challenge of design, then, is to support the work of engagement, imagination, and alignment" (Wenger, 1998, p. 237). He extends this argument in his most recent book in *Cultivating Communities of Practice* (Wenger et al., 2002), which is more of a how-to guide for organizations seeking to design communities of practice (Cox, 2005; Hall & Davenport, 2002). This underlying tension between how to design CoPs (prescriptive) and how to characterize existing CoPs (descriptive) is also found in the literature of organizational learning and learning organization (Tsang, 1997).

The study outlined in this book will describe both successful, and to varying degrees, less successful CoPs, especially within professions that are rapidly changing and/or for which there is a shortage of human resources. By providing "thick descriptions" (Geertz, 1973) of learning within communities of practice, this study will inform a variety of organizations that support professionals. While some organizations attempt to *create* online communities of practice and/or to set up online forums in which people can communicate with each other and exchange knowledge, insight, and know-how, I will show how intentionally-created online communities of practice that do not involve face-to-face communication and community-building efforts tend to be less active. Most importantly, this book will offer insights to practitioners and educators attempting to foster successful online communities of practice.

Chapter 3
Ethnographic Accounts of a Community of Practice in Square County

3.1 Public Defenders

> It's self-rewarding in that you know you are trying to help people through the system when they are in a tough time. Most of the people are not really bad people. They just made a mistake... and the knowledge that you have been able to help them out is in itself rewarding. (Jason, personal communication)

The above statement represents what many would consider the core philosophy of most public defenders. In 1963, the United States Supreme Court's decision in *Gideon v. Wainwright*, (372 U.S. 335) made it clear that people who are accused of committing crimes have the right to counsel in order to protect their constitutional rights.

> ... in our adversary system of criminal justice, any person hauled into court, who is too poor to hire a lawyer, cannot be assured a fair trial unless counsel is provided for him. This seems to us to be an obvious truth. Governments, both state and federal, quite properly spend vast sums of money to establish machinery to try defendants accused of crime. Lawyers to prosecute are everywhere deemed essential to protect the public's interest in an orderly society. Similarly, there are few defendants charged with crime, few indeed, who fail to hire the best lawyers they can get to prepare and present their defenses. That government hires lawyers to prosecute and defendants who have the money hire lawyers to defend are the strongest indications of the widespread belief that lawyers in criminal courts are necessities, not luxuries. (United States Supreme Court cited in ThisNation.com, n.d.)

Though they perform what some might consider a noble task, the public defenders' status is relatively low compared to other attorneys who work in private firms. In the film *Lethal Weapon 4*, there is a scene where a police officer is arresting a man, and the officer says, "You have a right to remain silent. You've got a right to hire an attorney. If you can't afford an attorney, we will provide you the dumbest fucking lawyer on the earth" (Donner, 1998). The "dumbest lawyer" referred to here is a court-appointed public defender. Yet, despite their low status, the public defenders I have studied continually strive to become better attorneys. This chapter illustrates their struggles and offers narratives of their practices in a professional community of practice. In attempting to determine the conditions necessary for the successful cultivation of a community of practice, I will present a comparative case study of the public defenders' offices in "Square" and "Circle" Counties.

I chose the first research site based on the previously stated definition of a community of practice, i.e., communities of practice are collaborative, informal networks that support professional practitioners in their efforts to develop shared understandings and engage in work-relevant knowledge building. Using this definition, I identified a community of practice at the Public Defender's Office in Square County. I then gained access to another Public Defender's Office in Circle County. The purpose of adding this second research site was to examine whether a similar community of practice existed, and given this, whether information and communication technologies (ICTs) supported informal learning among these public defenders.[1] While I had not considered the use of ICTs when selecting the first site, I felt it was important to choose a site that was using ICTs as a second site in order to study the impact of these technologies. Thus, the two criteria for the selection of the second site were: (1) that it be a similar organization to this first site, and (2) that the individuals at this second site use ICTs on a regular basis.

3.2 Site Description

The Public Defender's Office where I conducted my first study was located in a medium-sized Midwestern town in Square County, with a population of just under 100,000 residents. The office has seven attorneys who deal with criminal cases – five men and two women. Since all have been working for this office for more than six years, they know each other fairly well. In addition to the attorneys, there are two secretaries, two clerks, an office manager, and a college student working as an intern in the office. Since the office space is small, communication among the seven attorneys occurs frequently, but informally. They do not have regular meetings, but stay in touch with what their colleagues are doing by "keeping an ear open" (personal communication). In the past, they had had regular meetings, but when I first started my fieldwork there, I learned that these meetings had not been held for over 6 months due to scheduling difficulties. Part of the problem with scheduling resulted from their relatively heavy caseloads. Each attorney had approximately 140–150 active cases.

The case work was equally distributed. Six attorneys took roughly 15% of the cases and the seventh, the office manager, would take the remaining 10%. Of course, there were exceptions. For example, if someone had a murder case, or a similar case requiring additional attention, then that person might not pick up new cases while working on such a special, potentially time-consuming case.

The Square County Public Defender's Office is located in the Justice Building in the downtown area of the county seat. The building contains the probation office

---

[1] The public defenders in Square County interacted with each other face-to-face in almost all situations, whereas the public defenders in Circle County relied more on ICTs to communicate.

and the prosecutor's office, as well as the offices of judges, the public defender's office, and seven courtrooms.[2] In addition, a jail occupies the upper floors.

When people enter the Public Defender's Office, there is a waiting room for clients and a front office where a secretary arranges appointments, calls attorneys, and answers the phone. She assigns attorneys to clients on a rotating basis. Before assigning an attorney to a client, the secretary first asks, "Have you ever been a client here before?" If the answer is yes, then the secretary asks whether s/he remembers the attorney that advised him or her on their previous case. If the client does not remember, the office keeps records of this information and the secretary can look it up. In this way, the secretary is able to assign the person to the same attorney when appropriate. This system helps to foster a working relationship between respective clients and attorneys.

It is usually quite easy to distinguish between clients and attorneys because of the office dress code. Attorneys always wear suits, ties, or something formal, whereas most of their clients wear casual clothes, such as jeans and T-shirts, and look worried. Only a few clients dress formally. Many clients are teenagers. There are about ten chairs in the waiting room, and sometimes they are all taken. Beyond the waiting area is a common area, six individual attorneys' offices and a library. The seventh attorney does not have a separate office. Instead, he has a desk in an open space, surrounded by file cabinets.

The location of the Public Defender's Office places the attorneys in close proximity to everything they need – to their clients, to the judges, to the probation offices, to the prosecutor's office, and to the courts. Still, their office is relatively small compared to the probation office and the prosecutor's office. This disparity is one indication of the power struggles that exist within the justice building.

Sally, one of the attorneys in the office, commented that:

S:... The biggest disadvantage [in this office] is that we are cramped.... There is not enough room. If I were going to change one thing, it would be to give us more room to spread out because you know, something's happening in here [library], and my office is right there, and Mr. Ashton is stuck in the middle here because there is no room for the seventh office. And you know, it's just hard to work in such a small office; and the investigator is down there, and he doesn't really have his own office. He's just working behind books. And the secretaries are all smashed together out there. But that's the one thing I think we should profit from is having a little more space to spread out, and maybe that's one of the reasons we don't have more meetings. It's that we are so close all the time that it's like you have to gather together. (personal communication)

Put simply, the office does not have adequate space for everybody. For example, Thom Ashton, the seventh attorney in this office, does not have his own private office; but instead, has a desk set up behind a row of filing cabinets. As such, he uses the library for meetings with his clients. Sometimes his clients might talk about sensitive issues that other attorneys in the office should not overhear, and the library provides necessary privacy. If the library is already in use by other attorneys, Thom

---

[2] One of the seven courtrooms is very small, so when I asked an attorney how many courtrooms are in this building, he said, "Seven or six and a half."

must hunt down an empty office. However, as I describe later, the small office space is not necessarily a negative factor because it has helped to create a collaborative work environment.

3.3 What it is like to be a Public Defender

3.3.1 Public Defenders' Daily Practices

The public defenders' daily routines are determined by the court schedule. "We have a variety of hearings. Some are very informal. Some are more formal, like pre-sentencing, modifications, sentences, and trials" (Paul Linton, personal communication). The public defenders also spend a fair amount of time meeting with their clients prior to court appearances (either at the office or at the jail), filling out their own paperwork, and negotiating plea bargains with prosecutors.

Nick, who has been a public defender for about 13 years, characterized his work as "people handling." His comment below encapsulates the essence of a public defender's work:

> I do some [legal work], but most of my work is not legal [work]. Most of my work is just people handling. I have to handle my clients, take a look at the police reports, and so forth. I make some determination as to whether they are probably guilty or not. I know the court system. I have 150 open cases. They can't try all my cases. They can't take it to trial, so they are going to negotiate with me, so I negotiate plea agreements. I'll see the prosecutor for a certain agreement that my client might find acceptable. And I talk to my client's family; I talk to the probation officers; I talk to the police officer. It's all handing people. I talk to court reporters, judges. Say a judge doesn't like a particular plea agreement; then he can say, "No, we won't do that." But it's harder for the judge to say no if he kind of likes you. See? You get that type of stuff that you've got to keep working. You don't want to make anybody mad, and you want to appear like you know what you're talking about. And you want to know everybody, know who everybody is, know who has the power to do something. It's all people. Secretaries – I want to keep them happy. It's all people work. Very little lawyer work. To me, the lawyer work is going to trial, arguing cases to the jury, compiling the trial, doing legal research, legal issues that arise in a case. I spend less than 5% of my time doing that. I do not have to be an attorney in this job, except maybe 2 to 3 days per year. (personal communication)

For Nick, meeting with clients, prosecutors, and judges does not require excessive knowledge of courtroom procedure. The challenge, he stated, is keeping everybody happy.

To provide a more concrete picture of the work practices of public defenders, the following vignette is presented. It serves to illustrate the duties handled on a day-to-day basis, the working environment, and the concern of the public defenders for their clients.

On this particular day I arrived at the Public Defender's Office at 8:50 a.m. Vicky, one of the office secretaries, greeted me, and I told her that I would be shadowing Jason, an attorney who had been working at the office for approximately 9 years. I took a seat in the waiting room and noted that two people were already there – a

Caucasian male in his late 30's who had long hair and wore a pair of jeans and a light-colored denim shirt, and a Caucasian female who wore a pair of pants and a sweater and was about the same age as the man. Jason came into the waiting room from the back office and briefly talked to the two individuals, and then he and I returned to the back office. The man, I learned, was Jason's client. Jason asked me to follow him and said that the day was going to be "a little bit hectic." He showed me his daily calendar, which indicated that he had a number of cases on the court schedule.

Jason then explained to me that his first appointment was a sentencing, which meant that he, his client, and a prosecutor would go over a written history of the client that included information regarding the client's education, his criminal record, etc., and then the judge would sentence the defendant. While talking to me, he flipped through the document and murmured, "I hate when I see three pages of this [criminal record]." He then grabbed two red folders[3] and two blue ones. He had a stack of six files on his desk, but said that we would come back for them after a break.

He walked out to the waiting room to see his client, Matt. The woman in the waiting room was Matt's wife. A court reporter who happened to be there told Jason, "Do a good job. They are nice people." We all left the office and went to the courtroom where Matt's sentence would be determined.

The prosecutor and the judge were already there. Jason and Matt were seated next to each other. There was a microphone in front of them. The judge announced that the defendant would be called on first and asked Matt and Jason if there were any corrections to make to the record. Jason responded, "No."

Matt added, "... Now I have a house and a job."
Jason questioned Matt, "You were homeless before, weren't you?"
Matt responded to the judge, "Yes, your Honor. I do have a house now."
Jason told Matt, "Say whatever you want to say to the judge."

Matt started talking about his family – his two teenage children, aged 13 and 14 – and expressed his concerns for them while he would be in jail. The judge asked the prosecutor whether there were any questions to ask. The prosecutor asked Matt questions to confirm that everything in the client's written history was correct. For example, he asked Matt, "You stated previously that you were a user but had never been a dealer. Is that correct?" Matt said reluctantly, "That wasn't totally true." I had not known until then that this was a case about drugs. I was told later that cases involving illegal drugs were some of the most typical cases handled in the courts. The prosecutor went through Matt's criminal history. It was a way to demonstrate that Matt had committed crimes more than once in the past. Jason argued that his client had been trying to be a better citizen. He had a full-time job, a family with kids, a home, etc. The judge finally said, "Mr. Matt White, I'd like to find a way to

---

[3] In office operations, each folder contains an individual case. Also, there is a color-coding of file folders in this office. The red folders are felony cases, whereas the blue folders are misdemeanors. Also, the yellow folders are juveniles. Therefore, other people can immediately tell which cases an attorney is working on.

work with you. The problem is that your efforts are too little too late." The judge then pronounced sentence: Matt would serve 6 years in prison. If granted parole, he might be released in 3 years. Matt walked to his wife, who was sitting in an audience seat, and hugged her several times and kept telling her, "three years." Jason signed the necessary papers and began preparing for his next case.

Jason's next client, a man named Fred, was brought to the court. Fred was a 25-year-old Caucasian male already serving time in jail. The charges against Fred stemmed from contact he had made with his wife and children despite an order from the court forbidding him to do so. The judge asked whether Fred would agree to plead guilty and whether he understood the implications. He agreed to plead guilty and to give up the right to be silent, but he retained the right to have an attorney. Jason went through the paperwork with his client and confirmed the facts listed in the client's history with Fred. The judge then announced her decision: probation without supervision. She explained to Fred the difference between supervised probation and unsupervised probation. The judge ordered Fred to have no contact with his wife and children in the future. Jason went through the list of conditions with Fred and had him sign it.

After returning to the office, Jason stopped by the office to drop off some paperwork and check his mailbox. We then made our way to a different courtroom. This courtroom happened to be where Alisha and Sally, two other public defenders, were. They were sitting next to each other, going over the court schedule, and talking about a trial for one of Alisha's clients set for the following day. Alisha commented, "My kid [i.e., her client] is worried about tomorrow." Meanwhile Jason had begun talking to a court reporter in the room. Alisha then noticed her client, who was sitting next to me, and said with smile, "Bill, I didn't mean to ignore you. Come on over." Alisha was very friendly and went out of the courtroom with Bill to discuss his case.

After Alisha left, Jason sat down near Sally to wait for his client to show up in court. The court reporter that Jason had been talking with earlier mentioned that his client might be in a different court. Sally and Jason agreed, and Jason said, "That's possible." When the judge came in, everyone stood up and then was seated. From what I could ascertain, Jason's client had failed to appear.

Jason then had to go to yet another courtroom. As we entered the court, the judge called Jason over. Jason approached the bench and talked briefly with the judge. After that, Jason went through his files for about five minutes and then walked out of the courtroom with his client – a young Black woman in her early 30's named Naomi. I also noticed Nick sitting with his client on the right side of the room. His client, a Black man, perhaps 35, wore orange jail coveralls.

Soon Jason returned to the courtroom, spoke briefly with the prosecutor, and then sat down next to Nick, who had concluded arguing on behalf of his client. Thom came in and spent a moment talking to the prosecutor. Sally came in soon thereafter. I later learned that there are many occasions when attorneys are just waiting for their turn. Such times provide an opportunity for the public defenders to learn what the other attorneys are doing. Eventually, Jason and his client were called before the judge.

In this particular courtroom, two people (usually a client and an attorney) would go before the judge to discuss their case. Since the room was large, it was hard for me to hear what Jason and the judge were discussing. It appeared that Jason's case would be dealt with on a different day. He gestured to me that we should leave and mentioned later that "This [case] was taken care of for the moment." It was barely 10:30 a.m., and Jason had already handled three cases.

Back in the office Vicky informed Jason that a man had called and left a message saying that he would do whatever he could to help Matt pay his reparations. This was in reference to Jason's first case that day. Jason seemed to believe that the reason his client had been given a six-year sentence was because he could not pay reparations as part of the deal. Jason went into his office and called the man who had left the message. Apparently, it was Matt's employer. He explained to the person over the phone that "the judge basically said, 'too little too late.'" Jason then went back to the court to talk to the judge about the money, hoping that the judge might change her mind. However, the judge did not change the sentence. Jason seemed disappointed, but told the judge, "I just wanted to make sure." On our way back to the office, Jason commented that Matt could have been in prison for nine years. Still, Jason seemed frustrated with the outcome.

Jason and I returned to his office. He put one of his files away and said that the case was closed. He checked his voice mail, jotted down a few notes and returned one of the calls while looking at the clients' records on the computer. At one point, he stated to the person on the other end of the phone that "I'm sorry, but I've been busy and did not have time to talk to other people given the 20–30 cases I'm dealing with now."

Jason's next case was being heard in the large courtroom where he had been previously. I saw Thom and Sally from the Public Defender's Office there as well. Sally was with a client dressed in orange jail coveralls talking with the judge. Jason went to sit in one of the chairs up front. Behind him, Thom was talking to his client. Jason suddenly walked over to the prosecutor, had a brief talk, and came back to his seat. Then, Thom went over to the prosecutor.

Jason and his client, a woman named Naomi, were called and went up to the judge. After a brief discussion, a follow-up hearing was scheduled, and Jason walked out of the room with Naomi. He asked her a couple of questions and patted her shoulder. Naomi thanked him and went down the stairs toward the exit of the building.

We then went back to the office. Jason wrote down the schedule for Naomi's case on his calendar, then sat down at his computer and searched his clients' records. He pulled out a yellow notepad and took some notes but was interrupted by a phone call informing him that a client of his named Eddie was in the office. He grabbed a file folder, and we left his office.

Eddie was a Caucasian male in his late teens. Jason met Eddie in the waiting room and went back to the courtroom where we had seen Alisha and Sally that morning. I learned that Eddie was the client who had failed to appear at the appointed time. Jason went over Eddie's record with him and asked a few questions.

When Eddie was called by the judge, the judge asked him the reason why he was late. Eddie explained that he had had an accident the previous evening while driving a child to a hospital, and that he was unable to wake up that morning. The judge said, "In other words, you were sleeping when you were supposed to be here." The judge then commented on an apology Eddie had written to a police officer and asked Eddie the reason for the letter. (Apparently, Eddie exhibited offensive behavior toward the police officer.) The judge also went through Eddie's criminal history and asked, "What have you been in trouble with before?" Eddie tried to explain two previous cases. Jason pointed out that although Eddie had been in trouble before, these were simply cases of being in the wrong place at the wrong time. He pointed out that in one case, Eddie had been in a car with friends who had been smoking marijuana. The judge was unconvinced and finally announced, "Suspended one year and supervised for two years." The judge added, "You've got me worried. You have been in trouble before. Do you want to end up in jail?" Eddie replied, "No, sir." The judge said, "If you get into in trouble during probation, you'll end up in jail. Keep out of trouble, OK?" The tone of the judge's voice indicated that he had doubts about Eddie, and he probably figured that he'd be seeing more of him.

After we were out of court, Jason put his arm on Eddie's shoulder, gave him a couple of hugs, and asked, "Did he scare you?" Eddie shook his head from side to side in the negative. Jason asked him again, "You worried?" Eddie nodded his head in the affirmative. Jason said, "That's good. Worried is better than scared." Jason seemed to care about his clients a great deal, and from the little I had seen, the clients in the office definitely needed that kind of caring. It was almost noon at this point, and we decided to break for lunch.

The above provides a brief description of the events that occurred in the morning while observing an attorney's work practices. By the end of the day I was exhausted and could only imagine how Jason felt. He told me that the day had been busy, but it was not exceptional and could even have been busier.

3.3.2 Nature of Public Defenders' Job

Being a public defender is not an easy job, and the public perception of public defenders is not always favorable. Jason talked about the lack of community support: "You don't get many accolades from most of the community if you just say you work in a public defender's office [because] you're the ones who defend 'scum' " (personal communication). Despite the importance of their work, public defenders are not as respected as they feel they should be. Sally, another attorney, also commented on the difficulty of the job:

> It's a hard area to work in... You know, our clients are in jail, and they are facing prison time. Sometimes they come smelling like alcohol, and you know they keep coming back, and coming back for all the obvious reasons. You are their mother, their counselor, their confessor, and their attorney, and their therapist too. You're everything. And sometimes you don't want to be. (personal communication)

One can easily imagine how stressful their jobs can be. Jason confirmed that dealing with troublesome clients is very stressful:

> ... [the public perception of public defenders] just makes it harder when you deal with some of these people, [changes his voice to a mocking falsetto] "Oh, I've gotta public pretender. Oh, God, these people suck. I've heard all kinds of bad things about them." So, they come in with that attitude to begin with. It's kind of tough on a client-attorney privilege situation where you're trying to get information from them to help them, and they think all you are doing is scrutinizing when you ask them simple questions like, "Have you ever been convicted before?" [changes his voice again] "What's it to you?" "Well, it's kind of important. I need to know for future reference." I am dealing with these people, and I don't want to be the only one in the dark. Anyway, that happens and again, that's a public perception. (personal communication)

Another factor that makes their job difficult is the fact that public defenders are perceived as being subpar lawyers because they are obligated to defend the indigent, and they are unable to cut it as private attorneys. As Jason mentioned, when clients meet with public defenders they are already convinced they're dealing with someone who is not competent enough to work as a private attorney. But it is worth noting that this perception and the concomitant stigma attached to the profession serves to bind the public defenders together. In this way, they become a stronger team because they cannot afford not to help each other. I believe that this is one of the primary reasons that a community of practice formed among these attorneys.

3.4 Two Public Defenders' Trials

According to the interviews I conducted, attorneys are more likely to provide extra help to one another when someone is defending a client in a trial setting. I had the opportunity to observe two trials during my fieldwork. In both cases, I was in the office the day before the trial and sat in court during the trial. Prior to the trials that I observed, Sally described to me how attorneys in the office had helped each other, particularly when somebody was taking a case to trial.

> When someone has a trial, everyone tends to get involved. So, we just finished Alisha's 3-day rape trial that ended up with a misdemeanor battery plea... But everybody gets that sort of energizing time for the whole office. Everybody gets involved, if she needs help with something in the middle of the trial, if something comes up, everybody just sort of rallies. So, in that sense... the times we [work] the closest together are when someone is in a trial. We try to help each other out. (personal communication)

Sally's comments support the following observation: a trial encouraged attorneys in this office to collaborate with each other regardless of the fact that their work is highly individualized.

Preparing and arguing a case in trial is an extremely arduous task. It requires concentration, strategy, toughness under strong pressure, and at times, luck. Sally described what she calls "trial mode":

There is a T-shirt that I have seen that has a cat with its claws out like this, claws trying to hold on. All you see is these scratch marks down the wood. And the top says, "Trial Mode." And that's how you get. You just have to. Just that your adrenaline starts pumping and until you've had the experience, you think that you would have a heart attack and die. It starts about a week before the trial, and you just, your heart is, you can feel it pumping faster and you can feel your adrenaline going, and it just continues right though the trial until the end of the closing arguments and then your whole body sort of zzzz [mimics snoring]. But it's just a physiological thing.

I imagine that being in "trial mode" is akin to what professional athletes refer to as "putting on your game face" and serves as a means of psyching oneself up for a challenge – in this case, a trial. Even as a mere observer shadowing two attorneys, I found myself getting caught up in the excitement of the trial. Sally confirmed my thoughts: "It's a lot of work, when you think about it. It's like, it never leaves your mind. You dream about it." (personal communication)

Mary, a prosecutor, shared similar thoughts with me after I noted that Alisha looked different during the trial than she had at other times:

She is, and we probably all are to a certain degree. And some of it's probably intentional, that you're trying to make sure that you're very careful about the way you speak, and very professional and all that. But some of it's also unintentional because I'm sure my emotions are different when I'm in trial, and that may make me react differently. Like I'm more hyped up and excited when I'm in trial than on a daily basis. (personal communication)

Both Sally and Mary agreed that a trial is an energetic experience, and the support these attorneys give each other is crucial to their success and their ability to rise to the occasion when necessary. The key is the sense of community that exists in Square County Public Defender's Office.

3.4.1 Alisha's Trial

The following account provides a summary of my observations of the attorneys in the Public Defender's Office during the trial of one of Alisha's clients. One of my observations was conducted the day before the trial during Alisha's preparations for the trial. The bulk of the observations were conducted during the trial.

3.4.1.1 The Day before the Trial

Around 3:00 p.m., Alisha and Richard were talking to Bob, the office investigator, just outside of Richard's office. One of Bob's jobs is to help attorneys who have to go to trial conduct legal research. Richard, a fellow lawyer,[4] just happened to be in the office at that time. Alisha said to Richard as she patted Bob's shoulder, "[Bob] is helping me [with tomorrow's trial]." As Alisha, Richard, and Bob continued their

---

[4] Richard is an attorney in the Public Defender's Office and is also a general practitioner in a private firm.

conversation about Alisha's trial for the following day, she said to them, "I'm calm for this case." Alisha explained to me that the case involved charges of child molestation. Two young girls alleged that their father had molested them. The father, named Ben, had confessed on videotape. However, Ben later said that the police, in the process of gathering evidence, had coerced him into giving a false confession. Alisha stated that it "is just not pleasant to have this kind of case, especially when little girls are involved."

Later, I saw Sally sitting in a chair at Alisha's office. Even though I could not hear what they were talking about, they must have been talking about Alisha's case since attorneys generally prepare for a trial throughout the day on the day before a case goes to trial.

Around 5:00 p.m., Paul Linton, the office manager, prepared to leave. He wished Alisha good luck. Just then, Jason walked into her office. Alisha talked to Jason for a while and said, "I'll check the tape again." After Jason left, Alisha was the only one left working in the office. I could hear Alisha typing. Sally later related what is involved in preparing for a trial.

> Felonies usually take a long time; usually, at least a good week before [the trial], you are pretty much just thinking about that. Your desk is accumulating a pile, and you find yourself just making lots of notes and spending your nights writing about it. It escalates then as you get towards the last day or two before the trial. You are usually up late and doing preparation things. And during the trial you usually use every second you can to write down – jot down – issues or thoughts or whatever. Then, once it's up to the jury, then you just sort of, that's it. It's fun. (personal communication)

It appeared that the reasons Alisha had conversations with her colleagues were twofold: The first reason was to obtain opinions and different ideas from other attorneys, including the office investigator. For example, Richard did not have any responsibilities related to Alisha's case, and she did not ask for help; however, in this office, it is common for other attorneys to volunteer help to the other attorneys because they all know what it is like to defend a client in a trial setting as a public defender. This trial did not appear to be an easy case to defend. The other reason was simply to relieve the tension one often feels before going to the trial. Significantly, my observations confirmed that the other attorneys in the office were aware that Alisha was going to a trial.

3.4.1.2 Trial

The trial started with the selection of jurors. Since this was a sensitive case, each juror was asked questions individually before going through the process as a whole group. As a result, the selection of the jury took more than half of the day. Once the jury was selected, the trial started and witnesses were called by the prosecutor.

After questioning a couple of witnesses, the prosecutor was ready to show the videotape that Alisha had been concerned about. The prosecutor set a cart with a TV set and a VCR in front of the jurors in order to show them the videotape of Ben's confession. According to the public defenders I interviewed, it is not uncommon for clients to confess to police on camera, yet still insist on going to trial. The judge sat with the audience to see the videotape better. The detective who had been present when the confession was recorded remained sitting in an area designated for witnesses.

The prosecutor started the videotape. The tape showed Ben in a room with the detective and a woman from a child protection program. The detective was aggressive. He said that he knew that Ben had molested the children. The detective informed Ben that he had medical evidence confirming this. Although Ben kept repeating that he had not done it, the detective would not listen to him and asked him why he had done it. The detective raised his voice a few times. At that point, Ben's responses began to change. When the detective said, "You did it!" Ben replied, "Okay," instead of no. Then, the detective asked, "What do you mean by okay, yes or no?" Finally, Ben said, "Yes, I did it." He described when the activities had started and how he had done it. It appeared that Ben had indeed molested his daughters. After the videotape played, the judge called for a recess.

During the recess, Alisha walked toward me, and said, "Can I borrow you for a second?" Alisha looked very calm and was smiling, so I assumed that there was nothing wrong, but I did not understand why she needed me. We walked back to the Public Defender's Office together. She led me to the back office, looked squarely at me, and asked, "So, what did you think of the videotape?" I now understood why Alisha had wanted to talk to me. I thought for a second about how to answer the question. Sensing my hesitation she said, "You saw the videotape, right? Did you think he did it?" I had to tell her that it was fairly clear that he had done it regardless of the detective's behavior. However, I also told her that, in my opinion, the detective's aggressive questioning of Ben had not been appropriate. Alisha looked disappointed and told me, "I needed to hear that from somebody other than the people in this office." I felt sorry for her because the case appeared to be lost. Then, Bob and Richard came to Alisha and asked her how the trial was going. Alisha told them that the prosecutor had shown the videotape, and that she was still debating whether she should have Ben testify or not. Sally came in as Richard said, "If you don't put him up, you may have a chance to appeal later." Alisha seemed to agree with his opinion and said, "Okay." Then she added "I have called his sister. She will be here. I will just have her testify." Then, we left the office to go back to the courtroom.

During the trial recess, the other attorneys had been very helpful and had brainstormed ideas with Alisha. I speculate that one reason for this show of support was that the nature of the events was, in a sense, reciprocal. This time it was Alisha who was struggling to define a best course of action, but the next time it might be Richard. Also, since the other attorneys had had similar experiences (i.e. arguing a case before a jury), they empathized with Alisha's situation. In addition, Alisha may have been looking for a second opinion. For instance, because they were not the attorney arguing the case, they saw the case from a different perspective – one that may have been helpful to their co-worker.

After Ben's sister testified, the judge called another recess. The jurors retreated to their quarters. In the absence of the jurors, the judge, the prosecutor, and Alisha spoke briefly. Alisha asked the judge if she could be allowed some time with Ben alone. The judge allowed them to use a room behind the courtroom, and I assumed they discussed whether Ben should testify or not. About ten minutes later, they returned, and Alisha announced to the judge that Ben was going to testify. The judge then called the jurors back into the courtroom.

Ben took the stand, and Alisha asked him point blank whether he molested his children. Ben's confident answer was no. Alisha again asked the same question. Ben denied this once more saying, "No," adding affirmatively, "I've never child-molested anybody in my life!!!" This statement contradicted what the jury and the audience had seen on the videotape. I can only assume that Ben was so convinced of his innocence (or his ability to persuade) that he had insisted on testifying. After this question-and-answer session, the judge called for yet another recess. Because of Ben's contradictory responses and in the absence of the jurors, the judge, the prosecutor, and Alisha began discussing the trial. The prosecutor insisted that she wanted to call another witness who had allegedly been victimized by Ben in the past since the defendant was now arguing that he had never molested any children in his life. Alisha countered that based on legal precedent the judge should not allow another witness to be called – in this case, one who could give evidence of a past record of child molesting. The judge requested a copy of the decision that Alisha was citing, so she went back to the office to track down the citation.

Back in the office, Alisha went to Jason and quickly reported what had happened with Ben's testimony. Nick was about to leave the office (he was putting on his jacket) and overheard what Alisha was saying. Nick said, "[Ben] is a liar" and told Alisha, "You know, we have a saying that 'attorneys don't lose cases, clients do.'" That comment did not seem to help Alisha. Nick then asked who the prosecutor was, and Jason told him. Nick said, "Oh," with sympathy. Nick's reaction showed that the prosecutor might not be an easy person with whom to negotiate. Nick said, "Sorry, Alisha, there's nothing I can do at this point," and that he was going to leave. Alisha asked him about a case of his from 20 years ago. Nick went back to his office, turned the light on, and looked up a file in his filing cabinet for her. With a photocopy of the precedent she had cited in hand, the file from Nick, and a coffee cup, Alisha went back to the court.

The contents of Nick's file did not help Alisha much. Ben's testimony had hurt Alisha's case quite a bit. During the next recess, Alisha talked to the prosecutor. "I was very careful to ask [Ben] simple yes-no-questions, wasn't I?" she said with a frustrated tone. The prosecutor told her that she had been careful.

But the fact of the matter was that despite Richard's earlier advice, Alisha had decided to have Ben testify during the trial. I asked later why she had made this decision, and she explained to me:

> The client always has a right to choose, so we can advise a client not to testify, but we can't go against their wishes. And in this case, the client wanted to testify. What he [Richard] was advising was a strategy for an appellant review, not necessarily about what would make the case better at the trial level.

I asked her to further explain the difference between the strategies in a trial and the ones used during an appellant review:

There is a big difference. Some cases you know that you're probably going to lose, so you want to set up as many errors as possible, so that the appeal court would look at it, and may overturn the trial court, and you can get another shot at the trial. But it's hard to make clients think that way, and in this case, you know, he just wanted to testify because he thought he gets up there and clears everything up. So, obviously that's why it was nice having you listen to the videotape, so that you could give me an opinion about how you thought it was going. Because having someone in a courtroom, they can give you insight on whether or not you should advise your client to take the stand. So, it actually helps. And in my past trials, Jason sat there, and told me that there is no point to put my guy on, and it really helped. I told you, I did the retrial of the attempted murder. First time, we didn't put him on, and second time we didn't put him on. First time it went really well, and I don't think it would help it if we put him on. So, it's nice to have somebody listen (personal communication).

This interview excerpt illustrates that the final decision is always made by the attorney who is conducting the trial, no matter what other counsel has been offered by others, including the client. During a later interview, I asked her to elaborate on the situation:

I:[5] You talked to Nick during a recess, and Nick pulled out a file for you about a case 20 years ago. How did you know he had the file?

A: Nick usually is very good at legal argument, and he had done one of the cases previously, so I figured he would be able to give me some help on that.

I: Was it the same client?

A: No, it wasn't the same client. The issue had to do with prior allegations of molestation coming in because your client has been accused of other things. There used to be a rule called the depraved sexual instinct rule here in this state. It said that if your client has molested somebody before, the prosecutor could bring that in to show that he had a depraved sexual instinct. That goes against our rules of evidence, which says that usually you cannot show somebody committed a present crime by showing that he did it in the past because that's too prejudicial. Usually juries can't distinguish; if he did it then, he probably did it now. And child-molesting used to be an exception to that because the cases are so hard for the State to prove. So, Nick was one of the attorneys that actually did some fairly groundbreaking work on one of his cases on the depraved sexual instinct. He wasn't the attorney that ultimately had the case published and got the law overturned, but he actually made the same argument on one of his cases and got quoted in one of the cases later on saying he was on the right track and the law was just a little behind on it!

I wondered how Alisha had found out about this, and asked her. She replied:

A: We keep up with published cases by reading the advance sheets... And we usually know if anybody is doing a particularly important appeal, although not always because it is hard to keep up with whatever everybody is doing. But that was a fairly big case that he was involved in.

After all the testimony and evidence had been presented, Alisha looked exhausted. It was about 7:40 p.m., and the jury began deliberations. Since the beginning of the trial at eight o'clock that morning, she had spent nearly 12 hours working on her client's behalf. When we went back to the office, Jason was waiting for her. Alisha had told me before that the attorneys in this office usually wait on the verdict with each other. Last time Alisha had gone to trial, she had had to wait until 2:30 a.m.

---

[5] "I" refers to "interviewer."

Alisha looked back at me, said, "Thank you for your moral support," and told me that having someone with her during the trial was helpful. Sally had also stopped by several times to offer support to Alisha. Alisha told me that she wished this office had more attorneys, and that she could have had someone sitting through the whole trial with her. This would have afforded her with more opportunities for feedback and input. After three-and-a-half hours of waiting for the verdict, the jurors decided that the defendant, Ben, was guilty.

3.4.2 Nick's Trial

The observation of another trial shed light on the differences and similarities between the styles of two attorneys during two separate trials. This time I would be shadowing Nick. The following illustrates how Nick's co-workers offered him moral and professional support; it also shows that despite Nick's confidence, he was under quite a bit of pressure and faced a situation where he was not in a good position to defend his client. My focus here will be on three aspects of the trial: the dialogue between Nick and his colleagues, his competency as a public defender, and his concern for his client.

3.4.2.1 Day 1 of the Trial

I did not learn until the evening before the trial that Nick would be the attorney, so I was unable to observe Nick's preparations to the same degree that I had with Alisha. Nick would be defending a case concerning the distribution of more than 3 grams of cocaine on three separate occasions. The defendant had been charged with a Class A felony on each count. The prosecutor for this trial was a young attorney. In the courtroom, the judge explained trial procedure to the jurors. Unlike the judge in Alisha's trial, this judge stated very clearly how important it was to consider the defendant innocent until a verdict of guilty had been reached. The judge then posed a number of questions to the jurors. There were about 30 potential jurors, but only 12 would be selected (with usually two more being chosen to serve as alternates in case of juror disqualification). Sally, one of the attorneys from the Public Defender's Office, came in to observe the trial and left within 5 or 10 minutes. I later learned that the attorneys in this office usually show up in court when one of the attorneys is trying a case. It is one way that they show support for each other. Also, the attorneys mentioned that watching one of their own during a trial was educational. Therefore, a trial can serve as an informal learning opportunity for the other attorneys.

Around 12:15 p.m., the judge called a recess. When Nick and I went outside the courtroom, we noticed two men sitting on a bench who were waiting for the prosecutor. They joked with us and stated that although they had flown all the way from Chicago for him, the prosecutor did not take adequate care of them. Nick told them that the prosecutor was a bit nervous. During Alisha's trial, the level of her performance and the prosecutor's seemed to be about even. However, it appeared that the young prosecutor in Nick's case was not as capable or as at ease as Nick. Moreover, while Alisha mentioned that she struggled to maintain an awareness of the behavior of others when arguing a case, Nick was able to observe not only his own situation but also the prosecutor's nervousness.

Nick preferred to go home during lunch time, but he stopped by the office momentarily. Back in the office, Alisha was there and asked if there was anything she could do to help. Nick said no and seemed ready to leave; however, he then started talking to Alisha about his strategy, as well as the videotape in which Nick's client allegedly confessed to selling drugs. The prosecutor planned to show the videotape as evidence,[6] but Nick did not agree with the prosecutor's assertion that the videotape would prove his client guilty. According to him, his client just made a "statement" but did not confess. Nick also went into Paul's office and discussed with him how things were going. Having the opportunity to discuss strategies and issues during trials is one of the advantages of being an employee of this office.

3.4.2.2 Day 2 of the Trial

On the morning of the second day, the third witness, Detective Rogers, testified. He began by mentioning that he used confidential informants (CIs); in this case, Andrew Miller and his son. The prosecutor asked the Detective Rogers to locate the place where the drug exchanges had taken place. The prosecutor set up a large flip chart and displayed a hand-drawn map in order to clarify the location. The detective was very confident, and his testimony was convincing.

The situation for Nick's client was not looking good, and there was a short recess after this testimony. When Nick went back to the Public Defender's Office, none of the attorneys were there. However, Nick did not seem to care, and his mood was a bit dark. Perhaps this had something to do with the difficulty of the case. Nick said that he wanted to see some sunlight. He walked to Paul's office because that was the only place with a window looking outside. Unfortunately, it was a cloudy day, and there was not much sunlight. He seemed to calm a bit but mentioned that it was hard to defend somebody who was quite obviously guilty. He continued by saying, "I love it when I've got the facts, but this time I don't have any facts." Sally remarked on Nick's trial later:

> Sally: It's that when we are trying cases like Nick's where there isn't much issue, there isn't a lot to say. Basically you just sort of buckle down and do it. It's not exciting; it's not interesting; things are not happening. It's just sort of this is something you do, and you do the best you can. It's very difficult.
>
> I: It's discouraging, too.
>
> S: Very. Yes, it's hard to do those trials, but we all have to do them sometimes. You try to get yourself involved in it, but it's hard to do it when you know you have a good chance of losing it (personal communication).

---

[6] The prosecutor ended up not showing the videotape perhaps because it was hard to prove that the defendant confessed in the videotape.

One of the office clerks asked Nick who his witnesses were, and he replied that he did not have any other than the prosecutor's witnesses. He later told me that he tried to find some hole in the statements of these witnesses that would work for his client, but he could not find any. When we left the office, Nick said of the witnesses, "That [detective] might be the most damaging" because the detective was so confident about the defendant's drug dealings.

Still, during the cross-examination, Nick was able to show that the detective had not directly seen the defendant because the detective had waited in a car while the defendant was allegedly selling drugs to the CIs. The fourth witness was Andrew Miller, the informant. Again, the prosecutor asked Miller about the place where he had bought drugs from the defendant. His testimony was consistent with the detective's. He testified that he had bought drugs on three occasions from the defendant. He also mentioned that he had been wearing a microphone hooked to a recording device during his conversations with the defendant.

Meanwhile, Richard, Alisha, a secretary, and the Public Defender's Office administrator came into the courtroom. They left after a few moments, and then only the secretary, Vicky, remained. Next, the prosecutor offered two audiotapes that indicated the involvement of Mr. Miller, his son, and the defendant in the drug deal as evidence. The quality of the tapes was not good, and it was somewhat difficult to identify the defendant's voice in the tapes because he had rarely spoken during the exchange. After the two tapes were played, the judge called a recess. Nick went back to the office. Alisha asked him how he was doing. Nick said to her, "[My client] is scared." Alisha said, "If I were him, I would be too." Alisha and Nick's conversation indicated that they were concerned about the client's fate. I could also see that Alisha was trying to offer some support to Nick. Concern for clients is a common trait shared in this office, and it is consistent with the organization's mission: to defend the indigent. The attorneys in the office then asked Nick how many witnesses the State had yet to call to the stand. Nick told them that there were quite a few more; the other attorneys were sympathetic because it was obvious that Nick still had a long day ahead of him.

After we went back into the courtroom, Nick cross-examined Andrew Miller. The State often uses CIs as witnesses in drug cases, and CIs usually are (or recently have been) drug users themselves. It is important for the defendant's attorney to try to give the impression that a CI is not a reliable witness. Nick's skillful cross-examination revealed that the CI was unreliable as a witness, and that he had earned about $2,000 as an informant. Nick also found out during the cross-examination that Miller was taking prescription medication. Finally, it was revealed that the CI had been a middle-man for drug dealers and buyers for 3 to 4 months before becoming a CI, and that he was under probation.

The situation for Nick's client was getting better, and Nick seemed to sense this. During the lunch break, Nick asked me if I had noticed that Mr. Miller had exhibited abnormal behavior. It was apparent that Miller was working as a CI largely because of the financial incentive, and that he must have negotiated a deal with the prosecutor given his previous criminal record. It was obvious that despite the numerous obstacles, Nick was doing his best during the cross-examinations.

Even though the State lost some points during Nick's cross-examination of Miller, it had saved a more powerful witness for the end. A police officer was called to the stand. The officer wore his police uniform and his gun. The attorneys told me that having an officer wear his uniform was a technique that the State used so that the members of the jury would be more inclined to believe his testimony. It was revealed that after Miller had bought drugs from the defendant on two occasions, he took the officer along to corroborate the drug sale. Compared to Miller's testimony, which lacked credibility, the police officer's testimony seemed powerful enough to persuade jurors to believe that the defendant had been involved in selling drugs. When the prosecutor asked whether the defendant was the drug dealer, the officer stated that he was. Further, the prosecutor asked the officer to point to the individual he had seen selling the drugs; the officer pointed to the defendant. After this testimony, the prosecutor played the third tape that recorded the trade between the defendant and the officer. Again, the quality of the tape was poor, but it didn't seem to matter anymore.

After the police officer and two more witnesses testified, the judge called a recess. Nick made a quick trip back to the office, picked up a notepad, and began writing his thoughts down without talking to anybody else in the office. During a later interview, he explained that he does not tend to talk to other people during trials, even during the hours when court is not in session. I asked him why, and he stated, "Because they distract me. By the time you get to a trial, you're supposed to have a plan. To see somebody else who has a different idea during a trial messes things up, and I start double guessing" (personal communication).

Before returning to the courtroom, Nick asked Jason where Paul, the manager, was. Vicky, the secretary, who overhead this conversation, told them that he was in Triangle County. Nick seemed to want to talk to Paul before delivering his closing argument. I had noticed on previous occasions that Nick preferred to talk to Paul over anybody else in the office, and I suspect that this was because Paul had more experience than any other attorney in the office. In addition, they had both taken on more serious cases than the other attorneys, including homicide. However, when I later asked Nick about my assumptions, he was not cognizant of any deeper meaning regarding his desire to seek out Paul. Finally we left the office and returned to the courtroom. The secretaries and the office administrator from the Public Defender's Office came to listen to the final arguments. In court, the prosecutor showed a flip chart that summarized the judge's instructions to the jury and then presented his closing statement. The prosecutor's argument was clear, concise, and persuasive, although, to me, it did not seem forceful enough.

On the other hand, Nick's arguments were much more persuasive and powerful than the prosecutor's. Nick had made reference to specific examples that came up during the trial, but the prosecutor had more evidence, more witnesses, and apparently had a better chance to win.

The defense and prosecution each rested their case, and the jury adjourned to its quarters to deliberate. The judge acknowledged the good work of Nick and the prosecutor. Nick thanked him and stated that he would be outside for 20 minutes or so to get some fresh air. Nick then headed up to the office where he ran into Alisha.

While they were talking, Paul came to listen. It was like a debriefing session – Nick reporting to his colleagues what had transpired, what his decisions had been, and what he thought about the trial. He and Alisha talked about whether they should have had their clients testify. Nick had weighed that choice and could not really decide whether or not he had made the wiser choice. Alisha talked about her last such experience, and said that he had made the right decision.

I believe the time spent reflecting was useful for both Nick and Alisha because it allowed them to evaluate different strategies used during their trials. It also served an educational function in that they were able to share their own experiences and test out ideas with their peers. Additionally, the debriefing session provided moral support for Nick. The attorneys present told him that he had done his best. This informal gathering allowed Paul to conduct an informal evaluation of the attorneys. When I asked Paul about his method for evaluating attorneys, he replied:

> I don't have any formalized guidelines that I use to evaluate. So, a lot of it is listening to the attorneys; a lot of it is for me working on cases knowing that I need more time to work on the cases, so it's kind of like that. It's more than a gut reaction, but it's certainly not any formal thing where I check off. (personal communication)

Feedback is received from a number of sources – some formal, some informal. For example, the attorneys sometimes receive feedback from the bailiff who watches the defendants and facilitates court procedure during trials. After everybody else in the office had left, the bailiff stopped by and talked to Nick about his final argument. The bailiff said that he had been offended by Nick's final argument because Nick had criticized the government's authority and its actions; the bailiff was particularly bothered by Nick's use of examples relevant to the Japanese-American detainment camps during WWII as well as government censorship. Nick said that he had forgotten to bring his notes with him – basically, a laundry list of wrongful government actions – and had been forced to rely on memory. Nick showed him the list, and the bailiff told him that he was glad that Nick had not mentioned all of the examples on the list, as that would have offended him even more. Conversely, I felt that these actions were indicative of Nick's competence in defending his client. His final argument was very strong and provocative, so much so that even the bailiff, who thought the defendant guilty, came to Nick's office later to comment on the fact that Nick's closing argument had upset him. Nick's client obviously had a number of cards stacked against him, but Nick did not give up. In addition, when Nick came back from court, the office administrator, who was also listening to his final argument, mentioned that his presentation was excellent, and that his examples of excessive government control resonated with her. These examples show that an attorney's performance is always public and is often evaluated by everyone who watches the proceedings.

The bailiff also informed Nick that it would likely take at least another hour and a half for the jury to reach a verdict because they had just ordered food; however, Nick was confident that the jurors would reach a verdict by 8:00 p.m. because the Shape University basketball team had a game scheduled to begin at that time. Sally later commented on Nick's trial saying:

S: Nobody likes to lose.

I: That's true

S: You have no idea what it's like sitting next to a client and having the jury read the verdict and find it to be guilty. Even if you believe they are guilty in your heart, it's horrible. It's just, nobody wants that. It's just that your heart just sort of sinks down to your toes.

I: But do you have to do it?

S: Yes, sometimes you have to do it. You can tell them [clients] that they [the jurors] will probably find you [the client] guilty, but you can't take away their rights. Sometimes, they don't have any other choices. Sometimes they just think they can be persistent. You can somehow convince the jury to disregard the facts. And sometimes you spend more time trying to make them see what's going to happen, and sometimes there is no point because they are convinced they want a trial and that's that. So, fine, just do it (personal communication).

At 7:45 p.m., the judge came to the office and told Nick that the jurors had reached a verdict. Nick looked a bit nervous. It had taken them just under four hours. When we entered the court, the prosecutor, and the detective who had testified earlier were already present. Once everyone took their places, the jury foreman was asked to read the verdict.

On all three counts the jury had found the defendant "guilty." Nick looked disappointed. Even though he was fairly certain of the guilty verdict, he had still hoped for a different outcome. After we left the courtroom, Nick told me that the jury had been too hard on his client given the crime and that putting him in jail would cost the county a lot of money. He looked almost angry. I told him that he had done a great job despite the results. Still, Nick seemed despondent and mentioned that the judge would almost certainly give his client the maximum sentence for each count. I wondered if the jury knew what the consequences of three counts of a Class A felony would be.[7] Each count could result in a maximum 50-year sentence (i.e., 150 years in total). If so, Nick's client could potentially spend the rest of his life behind bars. I inferred that Nick's dedication to his client's case compounded his frustration with the trial's outcome.

3.4.3 Comparison of Two Trials (Commentary)

We can identify three emerging themes in this section: a collective effort on the behalf of the attorneys to do their best for their clients, professional (and, at times, emotional) dedication to clients, and a tendency to reflect upon and evaluate their respective performances. I thought it noteworthy that the attorneys in this office helped each other and provided support when they had to go to trial despite the lack of obligation to do so. Alisha explained her experience in obtaining and offering help in this office to me thusly: "Every time one of us goes to trial, if anybody needs something, we all drop everything to help them out" (personal communication). Both Alisha's and Nick's trials were difficult cases because the prosecutors had

---

[7] I asked Jason to clarify this point. He said that the jurors did not have to know the consequences because their job was to decide whether the defendant was guilty or not.

more substantial evidence than they had and, perhaps, because the jurors were less sympathetic to the defendants given the nature of their crimes. Obviously, there are many factors influencing the results of a trial, and the attorney's performance is just one of them; but both attorneys did their best to work on their clients' behalf.

The underlying philosophy behind doing the best one can for his or her client is based on the public defenders' belief that everybody, including the indigent, has to have the right to legal counsel and due process. Throughout the time I spent observing the attorneys, I was struck by their dedication and determination to do their best. The attorneys' attitudes toward their clients were respectful and caring, and they seemed to understand that they were their clients' only support within a complex legal system.

As described in both Alisha's and Nick's cases, the attorneys constantly reflect on their practices. Paul, the manager of the office said:

> ... obviously if you lose a case, you always wish you had done something different. That's one of the things you think about... "Is there anything you would've done differently?" If you think about it and say, "No, I might have done this, but I'm not sure it would have been any better." Then, I think you don't need to beat yourself to death because you don't know. It's one of the things like, "Do I put a client on the stage to testify?" If you don't, you think, "Oh, I lost because he didn't tell a story." If you do, you think, "He was such a terrible witness, why did I ever put him up there." (personal communication)

In both trials, Alisha and Nick debated whether or not they should have had their clients testify. Nick later explained that the reason he did not put his client on the witness stand was because if the prosecutor had asked the client whether the client had sold drugs, he would have had to have said "yes." Conversely, Alisha's client had testified, and he had perjured himself, which had eventually hurt her defense.

In terms of communication patterns, Alisha was inclined to talk with other attorneys, to bounce ideas off them, and to seek input and suggestions. She would also talk with the other attorneys during the trial whereas Nick preferred to be by himself. These behaviors are indicative of personal style as Alisha is, by nature, an out-going person, and Nick is more reserved. In the courtroom, Alisha tended to show her emotions more during the trial and to be slightly aggressive whereas Nick maintained a very calm demeanor. Regardless of the variations in their communication styles, each attorney did discuss the cases with the other attorneys – though to varying degrees.

Thom, another attorney in the office, mentioned that reflection was an essential aspect of a lawyer's routine. When I asked him whether he reflected on his own performance, he said:

> To me, it's a constant process. You always think about the last issue you had in front of a judge or a prosecutor. What can you do better, or what can I try this time that I didn't try last time, or something like that. It's not an organized fashion, or it's not like a meditation session or something where I say, "every day at 7:30 in the morning, I'm going to reflect for an hour." It's much more at night thinking about things... I always think about things, [but] I don't obsess about things as much as I used to. I think there's a difference between reflection and obsession, but I think it's constantly in your head – [what] you can do better or easier for different results. (personal communication)

Sally also remarked on her own tendency to reflect back on previous trials:

> You just think it back over, and often it comes up specifically with trials because you are always rethinking your strategies. But as you read cases, you think, gee, I could have argued that, or I should have tried to keep that statement out, or why didn't I think of this. So, you can't pick up a legal book with cases in it and read a case without having it remind you of something you did or didn't do. The more experience you have, it's a constant re-evaluation of everything you have done, which is good. (personal communication)

The attorneys' reflections are, of course, personal, but I occasionally observed the Square County public defenders sharing their reflections with their colleagues. When I asked Thom whether he shared his reflections with other attorneys, he replied, "Anecdotally, I mean, not in any organized fashion. And certain anecdotes for certain cases, yeah, we do. For... most of the time, it's just a personal reflection" (personal communication). As is evident, reflection is an important part of an attorney's work practice. Despite variations in style or approach, the attorneys in this office learn from their experiences and sometimes share their reflections and experiences with the other attorneys. Schön (1983) calls this "reflecting-in-practice" (p. 59). Although these attorneys may not explicitly share their personal reflections, as indicated in Thom's comment, their reflections are, in effect, embedded in the stories they tell each other.

Chapter 4
Characteristics of a Community of Practice in Square County

4.1 Introduction

To better understand the concept of communities of practice, we will look at attorney work practices in Square and Circle Counties within the context of six emerging themes in the communities of practice literature.[1] In doing so, we will consider new examples and place the vignettes from the previous chapter within the framework of these themes.

As was evident in the previous chapter, the attorneys in the Square County offices consistently strove to improve their legal skills despite modest formal compensation. They shared information with other attorneys, and in doing so, learned from each other. A stated motivation for improving work performance was derived from the value the attorneys placed in helping their clients. During the course of my observations, the attorneys stated on numerous occasions that money should not make a difference in protecting a person's rights. As stated previously, this is a core element of the mission of the Public Defender's Office. Within the context of this basic mission, attorneys define their own approach to the practice. Given this, the first theme to be examined is the autonomy that Square County's public defenders exhibited when working and learning.

The second theme is the way that collective knowledge was developed between the public defenders (i.e. how they shared knowledge about laws, previous cases, court schedule, and judges' moods in order to help each other's cases). The third theme I describe is professional pride, which results from the fact that public defenders are specialists in criminal law as opposed to civil law, and as a result, are often consulted by private attorneys who generally have less criminal trial experience. In addition, the specialized nature of the work helped to foster a shared identity among the attorneys in these offices. For example, one source of pride among the public defenders in Square County was the fact that private attorneys would call them for advice.

---

[1] The study of the "Circle" County Office will be described in Chapter 5.

Adversity is the fourth theme I will describe that is relevant to this study. According to the attorneys I spoke with, the common perception of public defenders, including that of their "indigent" clients is unfavorable. Even some of the clients of the public defenders I observed did not treat them with respect regardless of the fact that these attorneys were representing them in court. These prejudices can make it difficult to evaluate an attorney's performance. In addition, even though public defenders work for the government, other government employees perceive them as the "bad guys" because they defend perceived "victimizers" rather than victims; the prosecutors, conversely, are often viewed as "good guys." I could not help but notice that the attorneys in the Square County Office used the term "we" to describe themselves and "they" to describe other government employees. One of the attorneys characterized it this way: "We [public defenders] are the stepchildren who do dirty jobs." Because of a lack of support from outside of the office, their jobs can often be very stressful.

Despite observations regarding the collaborative nature of some of the work of these attorneys, the work is highly individualized. As such, the fifth theme that I will examine is the absence of formal support structures for teamwork. The Public Defender's Office is often struggling with a heavy case load, and its attorneys usually work on their own. There are occasions when two attorneys are assigned to one case, but such cases are the exception as the office cannot usually afford such luxuries given the overwhelming caseload. As a result, the decisions made regarding each case are determined by individual attorneys. In addition, there is no formal structure for information-exchange (i.e., scheduled meetings). Therefore, *on the surface*, it would seem there are no collaborative efforts among the attorneys.

Perhaps surprisingly (and crucial to our understanding of the sense of community that developed in this office), the culture of this office was actually very supportive. This is the sixth theme I will examine. Indeed, despite the fact that the attorneys worked individually with their own clients and dealt with constraints of confidentiality based on client-attorney privilege, these attorneys worked closely and learned together. Whenever possible, the attorneys were willing to share information and to help and support each other. I suspect that there are two factors that explain this culture of cooperation. One is that there is no competition among the attorneys. The organizational structure is very flat. There is one manager in the Public Defender's Office, but the rest of the attorneys are all equal in status. A second possible factor is the presence of a manager who, despite lacking a strong leadership style, still managed to keep the peace amongst the independent attorneys in the office.

The six themes described above are elaborated upon in the following sections and displayed in the concept map (see Fig. 4.1, Table 4.1).

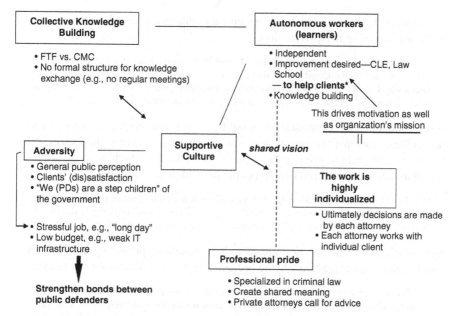

Fig. 4.1 Concept map of a community of practice in Square County

Table 4.1 Six themes emerged in a community of practice at Square County public defender's office

1. Autonomous Learners: Striving to Become Better Public Defenders
2. Collective Knowledge Building
3. Professional Pride
4. Adversity
5. Individualized Work Style and Personality
6. Unique Culture of the Office

4.2 Autonomous Learners: Striving to Become Better Public Defenders

One reason why the attorneys in Square County became public defenders was that they simply desired to help people, especially people who are not well served by the social system. This section will delve into the motivations and reasons that drove the attorneys in Square County to become public defenders. These men and women had other career choices, yet they choose to serve as public defenders, in part because of a sense of altruism. In the movie *Philadelphia* (1994), a former attorney was asked what he loved about the law. He replied, "Many things. But what I love the most about the law is that every now and again, not often, but occasionally, you get to be a part of *justice* being done. That really is quite a thrill when that happens." All the attorneys in the Square County Office, from what I observed, shared this belief.

Alisha explained her decision to become a public defender, which involved giving up a partnership in a private firm:

> I always wanted to be a public defender...I thought what people do in a public defender's office is to defend the Constitution, the underdogs. This is where I always wanted to be. That's why I went to law school. I actually gave up private practice for this. Don't make as much money, but I prefer this...I love this job. (personal communication)

In her comments, she expressed her belief that it was important to protect society's "underdogs" and that the money was not so important to her. I then specifically asked her if the reason she became a public defender had anything to do with the opportunities the job offered to help people in need. She confirmed:

> Yes, I like criminal law, and I think that basically you hopefully protect people and make them see that there are alternative ways of living their lives, instead of being in trouble all the time; although who knows whether that works. (personal communication)

Again, Alisha saw this job as a means to help people by protecting their constitutional rights. Nick explained why he became a public defender in similar terms:

> N: I have empathy with my clients. I can understand poor people. I can understand how poor people do things that society thinks are wrong. They need help. And I help them. That's all. I can help more people in one day doing this than anything I can think of. I like to help people, even poor people who are criminals.... I don't do it for the money. I don't do it for prestige. [laugh]
>
> I: No prestige?
>
> N: No prestige. Zero prestige on this job (personal communication).

Despite the unpleasant circumstances, all the attorneys in this office are dedicated to their jobs and feel that the profession is honorable, to varying degrees, because of the fact that no one else will help those who cannot afford a private attorney. When I mentioned this observation to Sally, she said, "If you realize that, then I think you have realized the essence of this job, basically. [The clients] need us." She continued, "They might be obnoxious sometimes, but for the most part, they are appreciative." She remarked further:

> It's a good job and it's rewarding, but it's also really interesting. You never know what is going to come into your office. So, it's never boring [laugh]. Never... If anything we are frazzled, but we're never bored, which is, you know, a lot to be said about the job. (personal communication)

The attorneys' motivation derives primarily from their desire to help their clients. The attorneys understand the financial straits their clients are in and expressed the opinion that it is important to protect the constitutional rights of an individual no matter how poor that person may be. As Sally pointed out, these attorneys also enjoy the challenge of their job. In addition, I found that one of the strong driving forces for them was to improve their skills and become autonomous learners – a pursuit that is facilitated, in part, by collegial input and support.

While formal education is necessary, attorneys in Square County emphasized the importance of informal learning via conversations with colleagues or observation of other attorneys at work.[2] The attorneys themselves make a sharp distinction between book knowledge and practical knowledge. Although book knowledge (i.e. factual knowledge like case law), is of obvious import, it is necessary to obtain practical knowledge in order to provide real-world context for book knowledge. In this office, the attorneys build their empirical knowledge base by sharing information and discussing the subtleties of their cases with other attorneys. This is obviously an informal process; that is, this practical knowledge is embedded in stories rich in situational context that is extremely difficult to index. Of course, one could argue that a complex database might help facilitate an effort to catalog this knowledge; but such a venture would exceed the fiscal resources of Square County's public defenders and overlook the importance of human interaction in the learning process.

4.2.1 Formal and Informal Learning Opportunities

In order to practice law in this state, all attorneys are required to take continuing legal education (CLE) credits. At least six hours must be completed per year and 36 hours must be completed in a three-year period (at least 3 of these 36 hours must be in legal ethics). The majority of the attorneys in Square County have positive views of CLE. For example, when I asked Sally whether she thought that CLE was a good learning opportunity, she agreed, stating:

> Yes, very much. It's hard to stay not only current, but on top of things in this profession because we have so many demands for us every single day by our clients, and by the courts. And so it's a way to just step back and sort of refresh yourself and get excited about something again, which is really good for us. (personal communication)

Sally indicated that CLE allows her to refocus and refresh since time spent in CLE classes gives her time away from the hustle and bustle of the public defender's offices. CLE classes also give her an opportunity to learn the most up-to-date techniques. Nick, on the other hand, does not think CLE is valuable:

> Everybody you talk to might give you an idea – an approach to a case or a tactic or technique. And that's what you might get out of a seminar; but is it worth driving there, paying money because it's a seminar, leaving at 7:00 in the morning and getting back at 6:00 at night, and sitting around basically for 8 hours a day listening to people who think they know more than you do in order to pick up a couple of tactics? I don't think so. (personal communication)

Nick's criticisms of CLE suggest a somewhat cynical attitude. In addition, he gave the impression that he would much prefer to pursue information on his own, to see to his professional development in his own way, and for the most part, on his own time. The other attorneys' views of CLE were mixed, yet, for the most part, positive.

---

[2] Of course, other opportunities exist for attorneys to obtain formal continuing education – for example, seminars provided by non-profit organizations that support professional development.

However, when questioned about the value of informal learning opportunities, all the attorneys stated that the value of these types of experiences should not be overlooked or downplayed. Thom explained that:

> We learn all the time. You go into court, and you wait for your hearings, and you watch other lawyers do their hearings before you. If there is a trial going on, and you have free time, you will try to go down and watch part of the trial to see what goes on. So, yeah, there are a lot of informal opportunities.

According to Thom, observation is a great learning process. When asked how people could discover opportunities for informal learning, Thom explained:

> There is a daily schedule posted...we believe experiential learning is the main method of learning here. So, we give you a case and say, "Okay, you are representing this person"... You go down to court, and while you are waiting for your hearing, you see other lawyers, you see them talk to prosecutors – how do they talk to prosecutors? See how they interact with the judge. You see where they stand (or they don't), where they sit, and all that stuff. So, you're sort of forced to [learn]. And...you learn to read the schedule, you sort of see, "Okay, there is a jury trial down in room 317 that looks interesting and has good lawyers trying the case. Oh, I've heard so and so is a good lawyer." So I go down and watch that. (personal communication)

Thom's explanation illustrates how both less and more experienced attorneys learn by interaction and observation. When asked how he assesses another attorney's reputation, he explained:

> Basically, you have to take some initiative in going around to other lawyers in the office and asking questions like, "What's this mean?" or asking [about] interpretations... Basically, you have to be self-motivated to start the process to be able to figure out the information. If you are not self-motivated, you are in trouble here in this office. You are in big trouble.

Of course, self-motivation is important in any profession. When I questioned Mary, an attorney in the prosecutor's office, she also mentioned the importance of being self-motivated. She explained that she gained her informal learning experience by watching other attorneys:

> I: I also noticed that the people from the prosecutor's office observed trials, too. They also learn from each other?
>
> M: You're learning from each other, and you're definitely learning from the defense. Generally, if I have got a jury trial coming up with a specific defense attorney that I haven't tried a case against before, and somebody else is going to try a case against him, I'll go up and watch that person's style, just to see if I can pick up on things that they do. Definitely, that's a great learning experience, I love to watch other attorneys practice...you learn a lot that way (personal communication).

Not surprisingly, Mary's comments confirmed that informal learning opportunities are common to both public defenders and prosecutors. In discussing trials in which she had gone up against Alisha, one of the public defenders, she stated:

> I could liken it [trial] to a sporting event. In that, when you do sports and you play a competitor that's really good, sometimes that makes you better. And then if you get better, they get better. It's kind of like that... that's part of the reason I really like to try cases with Alisha because Alisha is really good. She's a good one to learn from. (personal communication)

Here, Mary touches on the importance of learning by practice. Observing Alisha motivated her to improve. In this way, both become better attorneys. The allusion to an athletic contest is apropos. Indeed, challenges often bring out the best in an individual.

In the next section, I will discuss how formal and informal learning opportunities supplement each other.

4.2.2 Practical Knowledge versus Book Knowledge

All of the Square County office attorneys, including one of the prosecutors, differentiated between "book knowledge" learned in law school/seminars and "practical knowledge," in which information gleaned in these settings is put into practice in a real-world context. Expressed another way, book knowledge refers to an attorney's knowledge of statutes, policies, case histories, laws, precedents, and standards. Practical knowledge implies an understanding of when and how to apply book knowledge. The attorneys I interviewed stressed the primacy of "practical knowledge" over "book knowledge," though the former obviously draws on the latter. The process of conversion starts when an attorney begins to practice law. Paul, the manager of the Public Defender's Office in Square County, mentioned that a new lawyer, just out of law school, has "book knowledge" but needs to convert this general knowledge to contextualized "practical knowledge." Paul listed the first things that a new attorney must learn:

> As they practice, they need to learn what the particular judges think of different crimes. In other words, one judge might really dislike a burglary, for example, and another judge might be real hard on rapes; another judge might be really favorable of treatment for alcohol problems, or another one would like... to be able to send [all defendants] to jail or something. (personal communication)

Paul's observations regarding judges represent contextualized or practical knowledge because Paul was talking about specific judges in specific courts. This type of knowledge can be explicitly exchanged among attorneys.

I frequently observed that the attorneys in the office talked about different judges among themselves. They had to know the behavior, philosophy, and attitudes of seven judges in seven different courts. Obviously, this type of knowledge is not book knowledge; it is situational, and by extension, practical.

Thom described another kind of knowledge – intuitive, or tacit, knowledge:

> You have to know, for example, when to approach a judge, or when to approach a prosecutor with a certain problem or a certain circumstance. Or how to approach a judge; do I take a humorous approach, do I crack a joke before I walk up there, or do I take a serious approach? That's just intuitive. That comes from experience. You can't teach that to somebody. I can't tell you..."Now, see the judge's eyebrows twitching, that means ..." You know, I can't do that. It doesn't work that way. (personal communication)

Therefore, an attorney has to develop his or her own tacit understanding of the judges because it is not something that can be taught explicitly – rather, it is intuited over time.

In order to gain tacit knowledge, trial attorneys observe other attorneys in the courtroom. When Mary, one of the Square County prosecutors, mentioned that she learned informally by watching other attorneys in action, I asked her to explain the difference between watching trials and taking seminars:

> It's a different kind of learning because seminars are great for giving you academic knowledge. But watching people in trial is good for giving you kind of practical knowledge. And sometimes you learn a rule of law or the way you're supposed to do something in a seminar, but it doesn't really click mentally and make sense to you in a way that's tangible until you see somebody do it.

To illustrate this, she provided the following example:

> Let's say you go to a seminar on how to admit DNA evidence. And then you happen to get to observe a trial where someone is admitting DNA evidence, and you can sit there and put together all the academic things you've learned with even just simple things like how you move around the courtroom, [and] when you go up to the court reporter and have her put a sticker on something. When you show something to the judge, and when you show it to the defense counsel, and when you show it to the witness and how you do all those things; sometimes it's nice to actually watch someone do it before you have to do it... Unfortunately the first time I had to do DNA evidence, I hadn't had the opportunity to observe anyone else to do it. So that was just kind of, "I hope I'm doing this right!" I've read all the books I can read, and I've read all the cases I can read, and I've followed all the rules I can follow...now, I'm just going to see if it works, so that was different. (personal communication)

In the above scenario, the prosecutor differentiated between practical knowledge from academic knowledge – what I call "book knowledge." The process of converting academic knowledge to practical knowledge occurs by observing other attorneys' performances and matching their behavior with previously learned concepts.

In contrast to the prosecutor, who emphasized learning through observation, Alisha emphasized learning by practicing. She summarized the process of converting what she called "fundamental things" to practical knowledge by stating that "practice makes perfect in any kind of job." She elaborated:

> When you get out of law school, they teach you a lot of basics about legal issues. They don't teach you how to get up in front of a judge and say the right things, how to move around in a courtroom, how to pick a jury, how to do opening statements. Most of what you do in the beginning is you spend a lot of time writing everything out, so you know what to say...When I first started practicing in trials, I wrote most everything out so that I wouldn't forget anything, and I would remember everything I needed to do. And I still spend a lot of time writing, but I don't do it to nearly the extent that I did. Now I can pick a jury with my eyes closed for the most part, because I've done it so many times .... I would like to think that I'm only going to get better at it. (personal communication)

Alisha explained that as she practiced, she progressed from planning her speeches for the judge and/or jury to thinking on her feet, improvising, and writing out less ahead of time. She internalized the process and now selects a jury "with my eyes closed for the most part." Obviously, there is a stage when a successful attorney converts book knowledge to practical knowledge. This process of converting and interpreting book knowledge into practice can be achieved internally and/or collectively via interaction with other attorneys in either formal or informal settings. Given this, it is important to make a distinction between the individual conversion process and conversion processes that take place collectively through peer interactions.

Richard, a Square County public defender, described the process of applying book knowledge in practice. He recalled an experience during an earlier trial:

> I remember a rape trial I had, which was a major trial, 'A' felonies. I think this was a close call, and I never found my client guilty. And [he] was looking at 120 some years in jail ... I had this case completely planned out. This was one of the cases I had done an absolute detailed job getting ready for it. I had everything lined up for it. Every question I had, I read... This one book I read suggested I should do it this way... I know exactly every question I asked. I could refer to a page and a line number of where I was going to find answers of those. So I knew the detail of every single question. And I supposedly, when I asked the prosecutor, he said I cross-examined for six hours, I don't know if that's true, if it had taken that long, but it was a long cross-examination. (personal communication)

Richard remembered his case precisely because this is one of the cases he won by using a new technique that he learned from a book and then applied in the courtroom. However, he also acknowledged the assistance of his colleague Jason:

> It came down to the end where a decision was going to be based on whether my client wanted to testify and how I was going to do it. I remember going out of the courtroom and talking to Jason about this. He suggested a different alternative than I had thought before, and that was a lunch break so I struggled with that... And I finally took Jason's suggestion, gave it that way, and it worked out well. (personal communication)

Richard concluded that his victory was due not only to the cross-examination technique he had learned, but also to Jason's advice during the trial. In this case the collective effort of both attorneys was crucial. Jason later remarked on Richard's conversion of book knowledge that he had gained in a seminar into practical knowledge that he applied in the courtroom. He further commented, "... it's the best example that I know for continuing, trying to get better because he worked so hard" (personal communication).

Richard told me that he prepared for the case described above for four months. In the end, the jury could not reach a verdict on any of the charges, and it was declared "hung." As a result, Richard said that he and the prosecutor "eventually negotiated a plea to a D felony and on time served... I was very pleased about it" (personal communication). In this example, the conversion of book knowledge to practical knowledge was successful.

The data gathered in these interviews show that book knowledge is easier to share than practical knowledge. The reason for this boils down to the fact that book knowledge is always explicit, whereas practical knowledge can be either tacit or explicit. To better understand the difference between tacit and explicit practical knowledge, consider the following example: an attorney can gain a practical understanding of a judge's sentencing habits relevant to specific crimes via explicit information (e.g., historical court records), but to understand how to approach certain judges requires tacit (i.e. intuited, knowledge gathered over time via experience).[3] Still, despite the crucial role of practical knowledge in the workplace, book knowledge remains important. Richard, one of the Square County attorneys, made the following comment about the importance of theory/book knowledge to his work:

> What you are learning really is a method of thought, a method of approach, of analysis, on what other people have thought. So I think that is very critical because everything we do, that's related to it. We have to know the thinking. We have to know the process. We have to know the process of research. We have to know the theories behind the process in order to come up with good defenses sometimes. (personal communication)

According to Richard, both book knowledge and practical knowledge are equally important. This highlights the importance of blending these two types of knowledge (i.e., book knowledge and practical knowledge) that alone are less useful than the knowledge gained by combining the two. To this end, the attorneys in the Square County Offices build their knowledge base by sharing their reflections on failures and successes, by observing other attorneys, and by synthesizing these experiences with explicit knowledge to develop an informed practical approach to the profession. Because it is difficult to create formal opportunities for such a conversion, the presence of informal opportunities is crucial. Most often these learning opportunities are embedded in real-world situations as well as shared stories and anecdotes.

4.3 Collective Knowledge Building

In this section, I will examine how the Square County public defenders engage in collective knowledge building and what motivates them to work together. Allow me to begin by offering insight gleaned from a conversation with one of the attorneys. Richard described to me instances of how he had contributed to other attorneys' cases, in addition to pointing out how other attorneys had helped him when he was preparing for a trial. I asked him to elaborate and asked him specifically whether or not he shared information freely with his colleagues. Richard replied in the affirmative:

> I think we do that all the time. When I come across a good case, I copy it and give it to my colleagues, or just as I said, when I have a particular problem that I don't have an answer to, I talk to other attorneys about the trials. When I have a question about strategy, I sit down and talk to other attorneys. We also have an investigator here. He helps us, and I sit down and talk to him all the time about the strategy, etc. That's very, very important. So, we do that on a regular basis. (personal communication)

Here, Richard underscored the significance of exchanging information and discussing strategy with the other attorneys in his office. He offered two examples of the ways in which knowledge is shared between his colleagues: sharing citations and discussing legal strategy. He elaborated by stating that the process of working

---

[3] The latter is also described by Schön (1983) in the following manner: "the workaday life of the professional depends on tacit knowing-in-action" (p. 49).

with other attorneys in his office was rather informal. He brought up a case that he had been working on. He had asked his colleagues for input, and they had suggested talking to witnesses or tracking down the police report.[4] Richard also recalled an experience during a trial:

> I remember from the last major case in trial. I had my strategy developed. But before I called my client, I talked to Jason Kelly, and we discussed strategy. And he had a different idea, and I changed my strategy by including his. That's nice we have that. That's the big difference in some ways. I practiced by myself for many years privately and didn't have that opportunity … to share ideas and thoughts. Just have somebody to be a sounding board, bounce off ideas. (personal communication)

Even though Richard has been practicing law for about 25 years, he still considers discussing cases with colleagues to be of immense value. He went so far as to characterize the interactions he has with his colleagues as "partnerships." Although the attorneys do not work on the same cases together, the use of this term implied that there was a sense of shared interest in the work occurring in the Square County Office. Richard underscored the importance of having colleagues with whom he could talk to about cases by mentioning that he did not have these kinds of "partnerships" when he was in private practice. Jason, another Square County public defender, echoed Richard's remark about helping each other:

> I usually keep tabs on what's going on [in the office] … just general talking to find out who is doing what, big cases particularly. Sometimes not even big cases, sometimes little things come up. For example, a few months ago, there was a kind of a rule in a law concerning driving with a suspended license. Well, a case came down and said if a notice from the BMV [Bureau of Motor Vehicles] didn't include your right to additur [appeal] your review of the issue, then it wasn't a valid notice of suspension. Therefore, you couldn't be convicted of operating a vehicle with a suspended license because you have to have had the notice, valid notice. And they try to correct it by sending out a letter saying, "Oh, by the way," a month later. You also have to have the ability to have an additur review. Somebody has worked on that. Richard picked it up and shared it with us. I checked my files and I had 3 or 4 cases that fell under that category. So, I was able to get the cases dismissed based on the information I got from Richard… That happens, you know. Somebody gets something that's very insightful, and they share it with us - make copies and put them in our boxes or something if they don't have a chance to talk to us. (personal communication)

This anecdote illustrates the concern the attorneys share for the success of their colleagues. I asked Jason if this type of knowledge exchange happened often. He said, "Yeah, I think here it's pretty good because most everybody gets along, is willing and able to share with other people updates in a law or any other issues come up" (personal communication). His comment indicates that this kind of knowledge sharing is encouraged and supported by the culture of the office. Based on my own observations, I would say that all the attorneys in the Square County Office were supportive of each other.

I asked another of the attorneys, Thom, whether or not he was inclined to share information with his colleagues (e.g. if a certain judge would act a particular way for a specific kind of case). Thom provided another example of colleagues sharing practical knowledge with each other:

---

[4] This is similar to what I described about the trial in Section 3.5 of Chapter 3.

They probably know already, my colleagues I mean. We have a pretty experienced group here, so. But, what I might do is if I have a hearing first thing in the morning in front of the judge, and the judge is in a bad mood, what I'll do is come in, and I kind of make a comment if I see another lawyer leaving the office. I say, "Are you going to Gibson's court?" "Yes." "Be careful, Gibson is in a bad mood." We do that kind of thing. But there is no formal way. I mean I don't post a notice in the office and say, "Be aware all lawyers. Gibson is in a bad mood today." ... But we share things that way, and we share things, "Oh my god. Be careful. The prosecutor in Gibson's court is, oh boy, today is a bargain city. She is giving away everything today. So, you know, take your cases down and get a good plea bargain." We share that frequently. Every time we come back from court, we let other lawyers know that court's running behind or the court's on time, all that stuff. (personal communication)

This comment shows how the attorneys offer tips to each other via an informal exchange of "practical knowledge" about judges and prosecutors. Thom clarified by adding:

Usually, if they are getting up and got files in their hands and walking toward the door, then we know they are going somewhere. So, they might need that [a tip], but if they are sitting in their offices, doing work, maybe they don't care about court's time because they're not going to go to the court today. So, I don't want to bother them ... No, we don't go on a systematic basis and go to each lawyer and say, you know.

I: So, just when you see them going to court?

T: Yes. Or see them in a hallway or see them coming to court, or leaving court or something like that. Or, if we are in a court and they come in, they come up to us and say, "What's happening in here?" (personal communication)

These comments highlight the importance of proximity. As mentioned earlier, the office used by the Square County public defenders is small, so the attorneys cannot help but see each other when one of them goes to court. In addition, because all of the courtrooms are located in the same building, they often run into each other in the hallways; and because their work is equally distributed in all courts, they see each other in the courthouse frequently. Thus, their physical environment provides ample opportunity to share knowledge in informal contexts.

As is borne out by observations and interviews, the more meaningful exchanges of information and ideas occur on a one-to-one basis. This is partially due to the fact that the contents of the cases are sensitive and rarely discussed in public spaces; however, it also stems from the fact that it is easier for two individuals to discuss a case than for five or six. Richard mentioned that he often talked specifically to Jason before a trial. In addition, I often observed that an attorney might go to another's office to discuss a case; and I once saw Sally take Richard aside in the library, asking his opinion on whether she should take on a trial or not. Regardless, my interviews confirmed that these attorneys frequently talk to each other about their cases. In this way, they are collectively building their tacit knowledge base.

Thom confirmed that individual attorneys in the office are constantly honing their skills and building on existing knowledge. Thom said, "With every trial you do and every case you handle, you just get more and more experience and better." Because this conversion is most often an individual experience, I was curious to see how this individual knowledge became collective knowledge. I asked Thom whether the attorneys in the Square County Office were improving across the board. He stated,

"In our ways, when people gain some level of expertise, it gets shared somehow." I asked him to elaborate on how this process occurred, and Thom cited a case that Richard had handled:

> T: Well, for example, like Richard Wilson has a case where we're dealing with driver's license issues. And the notice that was required to be sent out by the Bureau of Motor Vehicles, you know.
>
> I: Oh, okay, I heard about that.
>
> T: So all of a sudden, people start asking Richard questions about that. Nick is another one who's done research on that. We could ask him, too... or Alisha, for example, will read advance sheets and will tell somebody about our case or something like that... Paul tried for a while to have staff meetings, like on every pay period Fridays... That would help kind of formalize some of the communication, and it would be a way to say things like that. Yeah, collectively, I definitely sense greater expertise in the office. (personal communication)

In addition to confirming the cultivation of collective knowledge in the office, Thom pondered instituting regular meetings in hopes of formalizing the process. I speculate, however, that a formal meeting may not be the most appropriate way to share certain types of knowledge because it can be perceived as a means for "forced" exchange of knowledge, which can sometimes do more harm than good. This concern was also addressed by Plaskoff (2003) who stated that organizations should not *require* employees to participate in communities of practice. Moreover, some types of knowledge (e.g. tacit knowledge) are difficult to share in formal settings. However, Richard would later echo Thom's attitude toward formal meetings:

> I think there is an opportunity and perhaps a need for some formalized sharing of information. As you and I talked about in the past, trying to explain how to use the LexisNexis. That would be useful. I've practiced in 25 years and as far as I know, I've *never* had the opportunity to work with anybody to have kind of formalized a structure of sharing of information. It's not like *L.A. Law* where each week they had a meeting, and they would talk about current cases. That's one way of doing it... It may have occurred. I think some people in some offices do that, have a meeting and talk about current cases. (personal communication)

Richard's comments reinforce my skepticism. Formalizing information sharing while of possible value, is of far less import than opportunities for informal exchange of ideas.

Aside from having opportunities for the formal exchange of information, Nick indicated that one of the reasons for collective effort among the attorneys was improvement of the office as a whole:

> Everybody watches us. I guess in one respect, you're working towards the standards of the office. You don't want to let any of the other attorneys in the office down. We want to do a good job. We all do a good job. We want people to think that public defenders do a good job. (personal communication)

Each attorney is a representative of the office. Given the pride these attorneys have in their station, the public defenders are motivated to work together to improve the reputation of the Public Defender's Office. One of the Square County prosecutors commented on the public defenders' drive to better themselves:

I think to a large degree they improve collectively because they pool their knowledge; not on an individual case because they don't work together usually on their individual cases... because I notice one will do it, and then all of them will start to do it ... Or they'll try a trial technique, and it will be effective, and they'll kind of teach the other ones. So, I think they have improved collectively. And that's great because if they improve collectively, usually it improves the prosecutors collectively; because when they step up and learn how to do something, we usually learn how to defend it. So we step up, and then maybe we learn a new prosecution technique which they learned how to respond to, and so we step each other up, repeatedly. So hopefully, if we're all motivated and we're all doing our jobs, we're teaching each other at the same time, which is great. (personal communication)

The prosecutor had observed collective knowledge building occurring among the public defenders. When one attorney tried a new technique or was given a new case, she stated that the other attorneys, in turn, learned from that attorney. As such, cultivation of tacit knowledge via knowledge sharing among the attorneys serves to support the mission of this office: to defend the indigent to the best of the attorneys' abilities. The prosecutor's comments address not only the collective effort among the public defenders to do their best, but also the influence these attorneys have on the prosecutors who work in the same courthouse.

This section has illustrated how informal information exchange takes place in the Public Defender's Office on a day-to-day basis. The attorneys help each other and collectively improve their practices. Furthermore, each attorney's work reflects on the reputation of the office. I believe that their efforts to become better attorneys stem, to a significant degree, from professional pride, which is the next theme to be discussed.

4.4 Professional Pride

As previously mentioned, the office provides no monetary incentive (beyond the employee's salary, of course) for attorneys to do well at their jobs. However, the attorneys all stated that the motivation to improve their performance should come from the inside, and that this drive is rooted in professional pride. When I asked Thom what kind of incentive system they have in the Square County Office, if any, he stated:

Well, nothing other than just personal pride, professional pride. Respect of your peers, the other attorneys ... But there's no incentive in terms of, nothing tangible. There's no money. There's no position hierarchy... you're better because you – it comes from inside. You know, it comes from wanting the respect of your peers. I think it's one of the ways we try to achieve that, by professional goals, becoming better. (personal communication)

In order to illustrate this, I present the following vignette.

One day I overheard Thom talking on the telephone with a client. He was saying to her that, indeed, Paul Linton *was* very good, but that Paul was busy. He then added that everyone else in the office was good, too. So, she shouldn't worry.

I asked Thom afterwards how he knew who was good. He mentioned that it was rather difficult to describe because everyone had a different style. However, he said,

"Everyone in this office is very good. That's why private attorneys call us to ask for advice." He elaborated:

> First of all, all the attorneys in this office are experienced. They have been doing this business for a long time. Second, being a good criminal lawyer, you have to do it all the time. You have to specialize in it. If you are practicing criminal law and at the same time practicing family law, and so on, you won't be any good. We only deal with criminal law; that's why we are here.

Thom explained that to develop expertise in criminal law is to specialize. Because of this specialization, the attorneys in the Public Defender's Office have to be on top of their game. Awareness of this fact leads to professional pride.

Thom continued, "To me, criminal law is the most important law. Seriously, whether somebody goes to jail or not is more important than anything else. Money is not that important. And people in this office think the same way. We share the same vision." Based on my observations, Thom's comments are representative of the public defenders in the Square County Office. These attorneys believe that practicing criminal law is the most important job in the legal profession, and this shared vision helps to create a sense of a community in the office.

As mentioned there is no formal reward system; rather, the attorneys in this office have to be self-motivated. Alisha explained how she motivates herself:

> I think the incentive is probably personal. We don't get paid any differently, based on our performance... I don't really see that at this level we need that kind of incentive. I tend to think that most people at this level probably do a better job because they want to; I'd like to be the best attorney I can be... Although, I don't know what Paul thinks about that; I think he likes that we all do our job, and he compliments us if we do ... And he frowns a lot, probably if we don't. (personal communication)

She confirmed that, yes, there is no monetary reward available. But she emphasized that, ideally, one's motivation should come from within. She does a good job because she wants to be the best she can be. In addition to the self-motivation that Alisha described, Richard explained the self-rewarding nature of the job:

> I think that's an internal motivation system; you want to do the best job. I think if you are asking me about the formal motivation system, there is none. I think in terms of working on this job and you go in and win a jury trial; you walk out and you feel satisfied, your client says you do a good job, I think that's a motivating factor. I think the motivating factor is when you see people in trouble that need help, and you can provide help for them; and I think that's another motivating factor. I think there is a motivating factor that if you do your job well, other people see that you do your job well and recognized [that] you do your job well. That's satisfying, and that's a motivating factor. (personal communication)

Richard listed three motivational factors that drive him professionally: achievement as its own reward, client comments, and other people's compliments. He considered his clients' appreciation the strongest motivating factor. When I asked him to elaborate on what he meant by "other people," he said:

> The ones I'm thinking of primarily I mean my colleagues, and other lawyers, people who work in the system who can perceive when a job is done well, and whose opinion you respect. And I also appreciate the clients when they acknowledge that you have done a good job, so I do appreciate that as well. (personal communication)

Richard indicated that an attorney's performance is usually public and is constantly being evaluated by other attorneys. This pressure to perform is obviously a driving force in an attorney's effort to provide good defense.

Mary, a prosecutor, confirmed:

M: ... it just seems like the public defenders end up in trial a lot more often than the private attorneys do, so, by and large, the public defenders are more experienced than the private attorneys [in criminal law].

I: But they have the reputation that public defenders are not good enough.

M: My experience has been that that reputation is not true... Now, that's not to say that there aren't certain public defenders, probably in certain locations, that are burned out or just overworked to the point where they just can't do a good job because they have too much work to do. But of the public defenders that I've worked with, I've found them to be very competent and among the best attorneys in any given area, and [they are] very passionate about what they do (personal communication).

Mary explained that the public defenders are usually the ones who have the most experience in criminal defense and verified that the attorneys' internal motivation stems from a real passion for their work.

The attorneys in the Square County Public Defender's Office are internally motivated to become better at what they do – what we might call "professional pride." A similar point is made by Wenger (1990) in his study of insurance claims processors. He said, "Most of them – and I would even venture to say all of them – care about doing a good job in a way that I found quite surprising considering the status of their position and reward structures they live by" (p.80). I would assert that professional pride is crucial to the cultivation of an effective community of practice primarily because one of the fundamental reasons for the formation of a community of practice is to improve oneself, to become better at one's chosen profession. Of course, motivation may come from external incentives like salary, but the attorneys in this Public Defender's Office placed far more emphasis on professional pride as their motivation for learning, in particular, from each other.[5] However, external forces, such as antagonistic clients and the negative public perception many have for the work public defenders do, can wear down this pride. The low status of public defenders is one of the themes that will be discussed in the next section.

4.5 Adversity

Public defenders sometimes have to work with difficult clients who may harbor irrational prejudices toward their abilities. As a result, measuring the successful

---

[5] The same is true of the claim processors in Wenger's study (1990) and Xerox technicians in Orr's study (1996). However, Wenger's case describes that there is an incentive system for claim processors because they have different salary scales based on their skills even though their salary increases seem to be small. On the other hand, Orr does not refer to an incentive system, and it appears that the Xerox technicians' organizational hierarchy is similar to the one in this Public Defender's Office, though there is not much of a hierarchy among the attorneys.

performance of a public defender can be complicated because a client may not be satisfied even though the attorney has done his or her best to acquire a better deal with the prosecutor and the court.

In this section, I will examine the challenge public defenders face when attempting to satisfy their clients' needs given the common (i.e., unfavorable) perception of their profession. I will also address how public defenders define success and failure within the shadow of their, one could argue, unjustified reputation.

4.5.1 Client (Dis)Satisfaction

When I asked Paul whether the attorneys in the Public Defender's Office are ever evaluated, he stated that there is no formal evaluation. However, he did mention that one of the main complaints made against these attorneys was that they failed to spend adequate time with their clients:

> For example, I and the office in general, don't do real well with what doctors call a bedside manner, holding hands. I am not real big on talking with people [clients], and saying, "Oh, I'm sorry. We'll take care of it." And talking to them – going to jail 2, 3 times a day, or 2, 3 times a week – I just don't do well for that. I think I do better just looking at a case and trying to evaluate it. And if we go to trial or something, I think I do okay. But, if you are analogizing the doctor thing, some doctors have a very good bedside manner. They are very empathetic with people. They make people feel good. Other doctors are very brusque. I've talked to some doctors, and they say, "Here is what's wrong with your father or mother, whoever, and here's what we're going to do." And they go do it ... And they may be the best person to do that operation, but that doesn't make the family feel good. (personal communication)

I asked Paul whether he had received constructive feedback relevant to the critique that the public defenders fail to meet with their clients frequently. Paul responded by elaborating on some feedback he had received in the past:

> You get some feedback because the family and/or the client contact the judge, and say "My attorney never talks to me." And the judge comes to me, and says, "Why don't you go talk to him?" So, I say, "Judge, what am I going to tell him? ... I haven't gotten the police report." Or "I've gotten the police report and gave it to him. And the trial is not until June, and I've talked to him 2 or 3 times to figure out what his side of the story is. I don't have time to go up there [jail] and say, "Oh, I'm sorry," or "It's a terrible case," or "We're going to win this" ... Yeah, you get some feedback and you try to go up there and talk to them [the clients] more when the judges say that. Other than that, I don't know any [particular feedback]. I think that's one of the biggest complaints from clients and families – that we don't talk to our clients enough, whether they are in jail or not, mostly when they are in jail. When they are out, they don't particularly want to talk to us... So, it would be better if we could go up there more often. [But] then we would have fewer cases we could deal with. (personal communication)

As Paul indicated, the overwhelming number of cases assigned to an individual attorney keeps the public defender busy and leaves little time for visiting clients in prison. Bob, an investigator in the office who used to visit the jail twice a week to meet clients, described his experience as an ambassador of the public defenders:

In some ways our attorneys feel hurt because they know how hard they've worked to help our clients, and our clients don't show respect, and that hurts. I get angry sometimes; I used to go up to the jail twice a week. I thought when I first came here one of the biggest things we had was a lot of tension building up between the attorneys and clients who were upstairs in the jail. The jail people will always write the judge that they didn't see their attorneys, you know. They want somebody up there holding their hand, telling them what's going on. Then, when they finally got to a meeting with an attorney, there was animosity from them, and they jumped in the attorney's face. As a go-between I thought I could alleviate some of it ... I kept that program going about 2 years, and I told Paul, I can't take any more abuse. I can't hold their hands, and I'm not going to sit there and listen to them talk about the people that I respect. (personal communication)

Both Paul's and Bob's remarks regarding client complaints are consistent with what Thom mentioned. When I overheard Thom saying on the phone that everybody in the office was competent, I asked him how he justified this given the above criticisms. He made several points and then said, "The only thing we don't do is 'babysitting'." Thom explained to me that "babysitting" meant visiting the jail, talking to clients, and telling them that everything was going to be okay. He said, "We don't do that so often, especially Paul." At that moment, Paul came out of his office and joined our conversation. We caught him up, and Thom told him that he didn't think he [Paul] babysat his clients much. Paul responded, saying, "I call it aging. I wait for them to be mature."

The following observations provide some insight into the individualized work, as opposed to the collective efforts described in the previous sections of this chapter, undertaken by the public defenders. The following vignette took place in the Square County jail and addresses the issue of how often public defenders meet with their clients and how it impacts client satisfaction.

One day I was sitting in the corner of the office when Thom suddenly asked me to venture over to the county jail. This seemed like a good idea – one which would allow me another view of the profession and provide greater context for my observations. On the way there, Thom mentioned that he sometimes found it difficult to visit clients in jail. "It's a pain to come up here," he said.

Entering the jail, we found ourselves in a dark hallway lined with cells. Everything was painted dark gray and smelled strange. We walked down the hallway for a short distance and went into a room labeled 'Conf 1' (conference room number one). The room was very small. In the middle of the room was a partition that allowed one to separate oneself from an inmate, if so desired. However, in all the times I accompanied attorneys to the jail, I had never seen a public defender use this partition. Usually, they sat and talked with their clients face-to-face. There were two chairs, and Thom asked one of the deputies to bring one more chair for me. While we were waiting for Thom's client, he explained the case to me. His client, Jim, was about 18 and had been in a gang. He had been charged with burglary but had not carried a weapon, which meant that he would be facing a lesser charge. Jim had been charged as an accomplice with another person.

When a police officer brought Jim in, Thom shook hands with him and introduced me as his intern. The room seemed very crowded after Jim entered. Thom started explaining to Jim the differences between a Class B and a Class C felony. If Jim agreed to the Class C, he could work while serving the jail time, but if he were charged with a Class B, he could not. Thom suggested that Jim agree to a deal with the prosecutor, so that he could obtain some work skills while serving his time. He seemed to understand Thom's suggestion and agreed. It was a quick meeting, and Thom flipped the switch to call a police officer. While they were waiting, Thom suggested to Jim that he think about attending college or a vocational school after serving his sentence. Jim replied, smiling, "I know." Then, an officer came and led Jim back to his cell.

After we left the jail, Thom noted that Jim had been well-behaved that day. When he had had a meeting with him previously, he had been rude and angry. I told Thom that he might have been scared. Thom agreed, and then said that he needed to stop and talk with the prosecutor, Mary. So, we went to a courtroom where she was working. Thom sat next to her and waited until she had finished talking to the judge. He then negotiated with her briefly. As we left the courtroom, Thom informed me that she had agreed to pursue a Class C felony against Jim instead of a Class B felony. I asked Thom if I could attend the pre-sentencing for Jim the next morning.

The next morning, Thom took me to the courtroom. The judge, Mary, two defendants, and two attorneys from the office, Nick and Richard, were already there. We took a seat and waited. While Mary was dealing with different cases, various defense attorneys came to her and negotiated deals. I was impressed by these prosecutors who could talk about different cases while arguing another case in court in front of a judge. While all of this was going on, Paul came in and talked to Nick. I now realized that this was how the attorneys communicated with each other outside the office: while waiting for their turn before the judge.

We were informed by the clerk that Jim would be brought over between 10:00 and 11:00 a.m., so we went back to the office. When we returned, we found Jim already in the back hallway of the court waiting with some other inmates. Thom again explained to him what the prosecutor was offering and told him that he believed it was a good deal. Jim listened quietly to Thom and requested a copy of the agreement. Thom made a copy of the sheet and gave it to Jim. Thom then made certain to tell Jim not to talk to anybody else (e.g. police officers) but himself.

Finally around 11:30 a.m., the judge called in Thom to discuss some issues relevant to Jim's case.[6] During this pre-sentencing, the judge indicated that Jim had written several letters to him. They expressed regret for his crime and asked for a lesser sentence. In addition, Jim had complained about his attorney, saying that Thom had not seen him frequently enough and had not adequately explained the situation to him. The judge then asked Jim if he now understood the situation and whether Thom had explained it clearly to him. Jim said that he did. The judge then indicated that sentencing would take place 12 days later.[7]

Later, Thom talked about some problems he had had with his clients, and I asked him about complaints like Jim's, that Thom had not visited him enough.

---

[6] Because of overscheduling, the delay of cases is common.

[7] Usually it requires 30 days before sentencing, but Jim waived that right.

T: When people pay me, one of the things that I do is I talk to them all the time.

I: You mentioned earlier "babysitting."

T: Yes, babysitting. That's exactly what it is. Now, some people would say that that's communication and that's keeping them informed of the process. I don't believe that's true. Because all I do is to reassure them, "Oh yes your case is, we're doing fine, you know, blah, blah, blah." And what I'd like to see us do is to rely more on interns or secretarial help... to go up to the jail, for example, and hold their hands, or just after we have to do the initial intake. But after we do that, then to go up and say, "Thom's worried and just wondering how you're doing, and stuff. Just want to let you know your pretrial is coming up. We sent your police reports, did you get them? Any questions about that? Okay, well, we'll put it up to Thom."

I asked Thom about Bob's regular visits to the jail in the past. He remembered and said:

T: Yes, they [the clients] don't want to talk to Bob. Yeah, that's a problem, too, but my feeling is that that's a public relations problem. We just tell them, "Look, I just can't get up here and see you as much as I want to, so it's going to be Bob that's coming up, or Noriko or Vikki or Tim, or whoever we have come up. They're my emissary; they're my agent, so anything you tell them will get to me." This is better than nothing ... Paul did that. But I think he [Paul] should do it again. It wasn't perfect, but I think there was some benefit in that. Because that's the single greatest complaint that people have about us – "My public defender didn't come to see me."

I then asked Thom about the letter Jim had written to the judge complaining about Thom's behavior. Thom remarked:

T: Yeah, Jim bitching at me. To some extent, when you get some experience in this, what happens is that the clients kind of get in the way of their cases.

I: What does [that] mean?

T: Well, if a client gets arrested, and I get the police report, then what I need to know is my client's response to that. What part of the police report he agrees with or disagrees with. But after I find that out, then I don't need them anymore. Then I can work on the case. But they don't like to hear that... So many times the clients decide that they have to lie to us; they have to tell us only what they think we want to hear. So the story evolves and changes and stuff. That's the hardest thing to deal with.

I: Okay. That's why you are worried about Jim's confession?

T: Yes, right. Like with Jim, when I finally went to see him, and we got over his initial anger, I'm talking to him. And he says no, he didn't talk to anybody. It was a case where there was just this one co-defendant's word against Jim's. That's a good case for us. We can take that to trial. But then I get the police reports and I find out Jim's confessed to an FBI agent. Why? And then he's mad at me when I write him a letter and say why didn't you tell me about this. Then he gets mad at me and says, "See, if you would have come up and seen me sooner, we could have gone to trial, and they never would have found out about this." Well, yeah, right, like they're going to forget about the confession. So, it's just that kind of stupidity I guess, more than anything. I don't know what. They're scared and they want to come up with ways to cope, and that's the way they do it. (personal communication)

At first, I did not completely understand the complicated dynamics that exist between public defenders and their clients. It seemed that sometimes the clients would betray their attorneys, in effect worsening their own situation by confessing to the police and by complaining about their attorneys. However, Jason explained that the clients were simply scared and frustrated and that as a result, they sometimes did unreasonable things. As Sally remarked, "You are their mother, their counselor, their confessor, their attorney, and their therapist too" (personal communication).

Thom's case concerning Jim Graham, discussed above, also draws attention to the highly individualized work of public defenders. In this particular case, Thom had no interaction with other attorneys because the case did not involve complex legal issues, nor did it require strategies like those required in actual trial proceedings. Because a public defender's work is so individualized, it seemed odd to me that the attorneys often collaborated with their colleagues. However, I soon realized that collaboration functioned primarily as an internal support mechanism.

Oftentimes clients are not cooperative, and the public defenders lose a high percentage of these cases. As such, it can be difficult to evaluate a public defender's performance; losing cases also puts public defenders at risk of having a low level of self-efficacy. "Perceived self-efficacy is concerned with judgments of how well one can execute courses of action required to deal with prospective situations" (Bandura, 1982, p. 122). It follows that in order to maintain a high level of self-efficacy, public defenders need the internal support mechanism supplied by collaboration with one another.

In the communities of practice literature, claim processors (Wenger, 1990) and Xerox's technicians (Orr, 1996) worked in similar ways. In the latter case, the technicians had their own territory that included the copy machines that they had to take care of. Sometimes technicians shared a territory, but usually only one technician visited a customer. Despite the individualized nature of the work, the technicians engaged in collective problem-solving, just like the Square County public defenders. Therefore, the people in a community of practice do not have to work collaboratively at all times in order to form a robust community of practice.

4.5.2 Criteria for Success

As mentioned above, it is difficult to evaluate a public defender's performance, so I asked the attorneys how they define success and failure. Richard compared being an attorney to being an athlete and characterized the difficulty of measuring performance:

> Sometimes you might try a case and lose, but you may have done very well . . . I think that's true with any kind of competitive environment. I mean if you play basketball, you may play an extremely good basketball game and still lose the game. I mean you did well, but you lost, and in some ways that's all that matters. So you feel lousy even if you have done your job well. No one likes to lose. (personal communication)

He also mentioned the reflective nature of the job, and said, "I think oftentimes we are our own harshest critic, and I think that it's a classic situation in our business and probably in many other businesses. When you do a job, you go back and second-guess yourself" (personal communication). Like other professionals, part of the public defenders' job is to reflect on their performance and identify means for improvement.[8]

Sometimes, it's difficult to articulate the process of the self evaluation. Nick stated that he knew when he had succeeded, but he could not explain how he determined whether or not he had succeeded. I asked whether he had criteria for judging performance, but his answer lacked identification of tangible measures:

> I *know* whether I am successful or not. I may lose a trial but still be successful because I did everything I could. Just because a guilty person gets convicted doesn't mean that I've done something wrong. Nor do I think it's my job to get guilty people off. I think my job is to protect their constitutional rights. It's my job to make the State prove beyond a reasonable doubt if that's what my client wants. That's my job to negotiate the best deal possible if that's what my client wants... You can always look back every time you do a case. You look back and think, "Oh, I could've done it differently." That's always true, but that doesn't necessarily mean the result would've been different ... Like I said, it's often difficult at the times when we have guilty clients. They often tell us they are guilty. You know they are guilty. What are you going to do? But I know how I did my job, just like when I mow my yard at home. I know whether I have done [it] right, or cut it too short, or too tall, or waited for too long, or, I just know. (personal communication)

I speculate that Nick was not able to clarify how to evaluate himself because he had internalized the evaluation process. Schön (1983) comments that "competent practitioners usually know more than they can say. They exhibit a kind of knowing-in-practice, most of which is tacit" (p. viii). Cook and Yanow (1996) reported on organizational learning in a flutemaking organization. The flutemakers there learned the know-how of creating sound instruments "not by being given explicit measurements and tolerances, but tacitly ... by working on flutes and having that work judged by the other flutemakers" (p. 444). Although neither Nick nor Richard clarified the criteria by which they measured their performance, they both made remarks that indicated that they regularly reflected on their practice.

Other attorneys in the office had other ways of determining whether a case was a success or a failure. Alisha described her method of evaluation in a slightly more concrete way:

> I think we all know enough about our jobs; we can probably have a good idea of how we're doing, based upon case results. How our clients do, whether they get a good deal or a bad deal, how people respond to you, how the judges respond to you, how prosecutors respond to you ... everybody charged with a B felony doesn't always get the same thing. But we don't do comparison among the different attorneys to see who's getting the better deal for a particular B felony. I think you get an idea if you're doing okay. And I don't think anybody has beaten up on me, so I guess I think I'm doing okay, and I think my clients do okay for the most part. I mean, this is the kind of job where it's not your result, it's your clients'. So if your client is satisfied with the result, and I think most of my clients are fairly satisfied, although there's sometimes when they're not, and there's not much I can do about it. This is one of those weird jobs that it's hard to define success. I mean, if you're a private attorney, you get lots of money, that's easy. But, I guess us still being here means that we must be doing okay. (personal communication)

---

[8] Schön (1983) discusses that this kind of ongoing reflection is frequently found in professional practice.

In her comments, Alisha expressed awareness of the perception others had of her performance (i.e., evaluation from judges' and clients' perspectives). Her criteria, too, are somewhat ambiguous, especially when compared to the following comments made by Jason who provided more objective means for measuring his performance. Jason called his method of evaluation a "rationalization":

> It's kind of a rationalization as opposed to intuition because if you can charge somebody with a fairly serious crime, you end up negotiating, for example, to a lot less serious crime, like they don't have jail time. That's kind of like a winning ... That's kind of like you have succeeded because ... before I started getting involved and where they end up are quite different. So that is like a victory and that's the rationalization I use. Obviously if you go to trial and they are acquitted. So, the jury says not guilty; well that's a slam dunk win. Wow. Although, I have gone to jury trials where that's happened, and I think "Jesus what a dumb jury" because I knew my client was as guilty as hell. In that respect, they should not have probably found not guilty. The prosecution just didn't do a good job. But I learned a long time ago. When I was a law clerk, I asked Nick, (at that time, I thought was dealing with a bad person), "What do you do in such a situation if you find something that might be able to get him off from whatever charge he had?" He said "Just do your job. And hope hell the prosecutor does his job. That's their problem." (personal communication)

Jason indicated that one of the criteria for assessing his own performance was whether or not his clients were charged with lesser offenses or received lighter sentences because of his efforts. By Jason's standards, his experience with the Matt White case in Section 3.4.1 of Chapter 3 and Thom's experience with the Jim Graham case in the previous section could be considered to be successes.

When I asked Paul, the manager, how he judges the performance of the attorneys in the office, he said that in addition to self-evaluation, he asks judges and clients their opinions because he feels that those opinions are of great value. However, he added, "... you can certainly ask [clients], although whether you can depend on their answers is questionable because we might get them a real good deal. And they don't like it because they still go to jail or something" (personal communication). Hence, determining success or failure is a complicated matter for these attorneys because one cannot simply equate losing a case with failure.

> Nick mentioned that nobody likes to lose, but:
>
> If you can't stand losing, this [being a public defender] is a wrong job to be in. You've got people who have confessed three times and have 5 eyewitnesses, and were caught with the goods. What are you going to do? You lose, but you don't really lose if you do a good job.

His comments puzzled me, so I asked him for clarification:

> You might lose the case. But you did not want to take it [losing] personally unless you did not do a good job. You can't feel bad because your client was found guilty and your client has to go to jail. You can't feel bad over that. You feel bad if you did poorly.

We can therefore assume that public defenders have to evaluate their performance based factors other than the outcomes of their cases. First, they self-evaluate. In addition, they rely on each other for feedback, and as Paul mentioned, the attorneys do get some feedback from clients. However, such feedback is not always reliable, whereas feedback from colleagues is more reliable because of their collegial relationship.

4.5.3 Commentary

The public defenders' positions are replete with negatives to be overcome. Their clients complain about them, their chances of winning cases are worse than the prosecutors, and there is no formal incentive system for better performance. However, the attorneys are driven to do their best and have established their own criteria for success, which are not necessarily related to winning the cases.

Typically, if a public defender ends up with a better deal than what the prosecutor originally offered, they consider their performance to be a success regardless of whether or not they actually won the case. Nick believed that the prosecutor in the case described in Section 3.5.2 of Chapter 3 did not perform as well as expected. He mentioned that if the prosecution had not had the police officer as a witness, he might have won the trial. In fact, the jurors spent four hours discussing the first two counts, situations in which the witness could not give any visual testimony regarding the defendant. Thanks to Nick's efforts, the jurors seemed to perceive the weakness of the testimony of the prosecution's witnesses in general, except for that of the police officer. This example shows that losing a case does not necessarily indicate that the public defender's performance was poorer than that of the prosecution.

The Square County public defenders remain motivated *despite* having a better chance of losing than of winning a given case, and despite their clients' lack of respect. Both Richard's and Alisha's earlier comments confirm that they are internally motivated, not externally. In addition, the motivation to become better attorneys, by and large, derives from the public defenders' desire to help their clients. This is one of the emerging themes in this study, as was discussed earlier in this chapter and is displayed in the concept map (Fig. 4.1).

4.6 Individualized Work Style and Personality

The presence of a supportive culture in the Square County Public Defender's Office should not necessarily be taken as evidence that the attorneys have similar work styles. In fact, the opposite is true: each attorney has an individualized work style and personality. Bob, the legal investigator working with all of the attorneys, shared his observations with me, saying, "They all have their own unique style. They all do exactly what works for them." He recalled an experience when first starting work in the office, and said, "I had to find out, basically learn, how each attorney likes to work: ... Alisha may do something, Paul may do something differently, all have their own style, and we all have to do what works for us" (personal communication). To accommodate the attorneys, Bob adjusts his way of working to suit each style.

Thom had a unique way of describing the different work styles and personalities among the attorneys. I asked him about the unique personalities in the office:

T: We're all odd balls ... flakes, screw balls. To some extent, some of us more than others, we tend to be pretty irreverent. Alisha and Sally are probably the attorneys that are the most amenable, or the most approachable, if you're from outside the office. Richard is not bad in that. Nick, Jason, and I are the worst. And Paul's even worse than we are, in his own way.

I: You mean, for a client?

T: No, just in terms of our attitudes. For example, I believe in this system that respect is earned. It's not awarded. And until you earn my respect, I'm not going to treat you with respect. And I don't expect you to treat me with respect until I earn it. And that applies whether you're a judge or whether you're a lawyer or whoever you are. There are people – Alisha is like this, I think Sally is, and I think Richard is to some extent - who want to avoid conflict at all costs. So, for example ... if they sense there's conflict, they'll try and smooth it over. Jason, Nick, and I don't operate that way. You don't like me; that's fine. I don't care... One of the best compliments someone paid me is a couple of weeks ago, a psychiatrist from the mental health center was talking, and somehow they mentioned, oh, they think that Thom Ashton is a real asshole.

I: What?

T: Because of the way I treated her. Because of the way I questioned this one psychiatrist in a mental health commitment hearing. Well, I consider that one of the highest compliments I could receive. I'm really proud of that.

Thom clarified why he considered being called "a real asshole" a compliment:

Because, what it means is that I was being aggressive. It means that the doctor assumed that ... we were just going to say, "Oh, doctor, just tell us, share your knowledge with us. And we'll just be in awe of you" ... If she's got opinions, then I want to know why she has those opinions; what's the basis for it. Until she earns my respect, I'm not going to treat her with respect. I will treat her the way I treat other witnesses. So, I am not going to treat her worse, but I'm not going to treat her different at all ... We are sort of unpredictable, so they don't know what we are going to do. And to me, it's just again, it's a respect issue. If somebody can walk over me, or intimidate me, then, they're going to intimidate my client. My client will get screwed. And I don't want all that to happen ... That's why you probably won't see Jason, Nick, and I being asked to join any of the big prestigious law firms in Square County. No, because they're afraid of us. They're afraid of how we'll act, they're afraid that we speak our minds. (personal communication)

Although the defiant styles of some of the attorneys in this office might prevent them from fitting in at a large, private law firm, Thom believed his style would protect his clients. He elaborated on his peculiar style of relating to his clients:

I also tell clients, if you pay me $5,000 to represent you in a case, basically you are paying me to hold your hands and to be nice to you. I'll try to be nice to you even if you don't pay me, but what I'm also going to do is just to be very honest. Because unlike a prosecutor, I don't have to earn money. And I think it's a liberating part of our relationship if I could just be honest and say, "Noriko, you're going to prison for 20 years. This case sucks. You have 5 eyewitnesses who watched you do it, and you confessed." And you might not want to hear that, you know. You might want to pay somebody $10,000 who's going to tell you, "Oh, we've got a case here. We'll try to get that confession suppressed, and we'll try to show these five witnesses are all on drugs" or something like this. And maybe they were, but that's something we'd find out, too. You know, the bottom line is that I'm going to tell you the truth, which is we've got our work cut out for us because this is a dumb case. And people don't want to hear about that. And people are always saying that "Oh, I have a public defender. That's why I pled guilty" and stuff like that. That might be true in other places, but not here because if somebody pled guilty, that's generally because they wanted to. That was the only option left. (personal communication)

In the above comment, Thom portrays his direct style of communication in general terms. However, being honest with clients sometimes gets him into trouble. Thom recalled an experience with one of his clients.

> I'll never forget. I had a client many years ago, about 10 years ago. He was in jail for drunk driving, and I won a scholarship to go to a trial treating seminar for a week up in Chicago. It turns out that when I was going to go for the week, his case was set for a trial. And he was in jail, so he had a speed trial motion in file. Obviously if he wanted me to do the case, he had to drop this speed trial motion, and he didn't. He was sick in jail. So, I said to him, "Okay, Steve. I'll get you another attorney in the office. You can have your pick of your attorneys." And he ended up choosing an attorney, and I came back from Chicago, and asked what happened to Steve. And they said, "Steve pled guilty." I said, "What?" Well, a prosecutor came in and made him an offer he couldn't refuse. He [the prosecutor] said, "We'll release you from jail, put you on probation, you know, no more time." Steve's record was like this long [Thom opened up his arms to show me how long it was].

While Steve decided to take the prosecutor's offer, he later had to go through the Public Defender's Office again because he had been charged with a new felony, driving while intoxicated. When Thom saw Steve again, Thom said to him, "You stupid son-of-a-bitch! You dumb shit! You pled guilty for something you weren't guilty of!" and asked Steve why he had pled guilty. Steve explained that he was scared because he was assigned to a different public defender. Thom continued:

> I said [to Steve], "It [the defense attorney] didn't need to be me. We had somebody better. You stupid son-of-a-bitch. You know, now you start with a felony." So, Steve wrote the disciplinary commission on me. And he said [it] exactly the way I told him. The disciplinary commission laughed and said no problem. So, he didn't like me telling him that, but that was true. He got scared and made a stupid mistake and screwed it. So, that's the something I think people don't like – our honesty. (personal communication)

The above comment illustrates an occasional consequence of brute honesty. It can upset clients, and in the above case, Thom was formally accused of being rude. Thom later said that he had not felt comfortable in his previous job because his boss did not "appreciate" his abrupt way of interacting with the clients. Although it is important to be honest with clients, Thom's style seemed extreme. Bob analyzed Thom's style:

> Thom will do outrageous things to protect his clients. He will push things to the limit. He'll go beyond that... He would go to whatever length it took to accomplish what he had to accomplish. He probably will push harder than some attorneys. That doesn't mean that he's more successful. That's just his style. (personal communication)

In this office, however, everyone seemed to accept Thom's working style.

I would speculate that there may be a reason for attorneys to sometimes behave in an extreme fashion. When I asked Nick about the prosecutor's performance during his trial, he mentioned that the prosecutor acted like an ordinary person during the trial, and because of that, he was not an effective trial attorney. Nick explained the gist of being a trial attorney:

> You have to have an ego to do this job ... you can't be sensitive. You can't go home and cry every time somebody says something bad about you or something bad happens here today. You've got to be tough skinned... You've got to think you're better than the next guy. I think

you need that to survive. I don't think I'm better than anybody else, okay? But that's the attitude you need when you walk into a courtroom; pump yourself up... When you go in a courtroom, you darn well better feel like you're better than anybody else in there. You have to put on that suit of armor, that charade ... You have to make other people think – jurors and everybody else – you know what you're doing. (personal communication)

Nick's description emphasizes the need for attorneys to change their attitudes, especially while in court. This characterization resonates with what Sally described as "trial mode" on p. 33 in Chapter 3. Mary, a prosecutor, commented on the divergent styles of the trial attorneys she had encountered:

You watch a million different attorneys do things, and you pick things that you like about all of them, but you still have to be yourself when you get in the courtroom. And you still have to do things in a way that is comfortable for you because if you don't, it shows, and you come across to the jury as being fake and disingenuous. And I don't think they respond well to that. (personal communication)

I suspect that the public defenders I observed had established their own styles as a means for handling difficult cases. The demanding nature of the job can wear on an individual. But a style, or mode of behavior, can provide an attorney with an alternate personality. When the need arises, they slip into this mode – just as Clark Kent becomes Superman – and rise to the day-to-day challenges of the profession.

4.7 Unique Culture of the Office

This section addresses the question, "What is the culture of the community of practice in the Square County Public Defender's Office?" The following three components characterize the culture of the Square County Office: the presence of supportive peer attorneys, a supportive office manager whose style allows for a significant level of autonomy, and the grim reality that despite the existence of a supportive culture, there are, as one might expect, times when not everyone gets along. Crucial to the culture is the office manager. The office's manager is the one who works to foster a friendly atmosphere, respects the autonomy of the individual attorneys, and helps to create the supportive culture in the office despite the independence and unique personalities of the disparate public defenders.

4.7.1 Supportive Culture

As described earlier, the Square County attorneys respect and support each other. This supportive culture was highlighted in Section 3.5 of Chapter 3 in the context of the two trials handled by Alisha and Nick. However, the Square County public defenders help each other in many contexts other than trials. Sally recalled an experience that occurred when she was new to the office:

S: When I was a new attorney coming out of law school ... in 1991, there was more of that [getting feedback from colleagues], and it wasn't just Paul, it was everyone who said you need to do more trials ... because I didn't do a trial for my first year ... And they [the other attorneys] were right. I did need to do more trials, and then I started to do more trials ... So, as a young attorney, I got a lot more feedback than I do now. We don't really criticize each other. But again, that's because we are all experienced attorneys now ...

I: But would they for somebody new to this office?

S: They would, yes. Because what one of us does reflects on everybody else (personal communication).

In the above interaction, Sally expresses the fear she felt when going to trial when first beginning as a new attorney in the office. Furthermore, her comments indicate that she received ample advice from her colleagues at the time. The other attorneys in the office helped her understand what was expected of a public defender, including the importance of going to trial. She also makes an important point in highlighting the fact that an attorney's performance reflects upon the reputation of the Public Defender's Office as a whole. When asked what would happen if somebody came to work at this office straight out of law school, Nick echoed Sally's reflections:

We'll all help them. Sally came in here like that. This was the first job she had [as an attorney]. We all watched and commented, and she didn't do the hard cases at first. She turned out real good, I think. Anytime someone comes to us with questions, we answer it, try to help. (personal communication)

The process of learning how to cope with fear is also discussed in Becker's (1960) study of communities of marijuana users. Becker illustrates how experienced marijuana users teach novices how to redefine the frightening experience as pleasure. An experienced marijuana user "teaches the new user that he can 'get to like it after awhile'" (p. 55) and tells stories about his own experience as a novice user. Sally went through a similar process as a new attorney in conquering her fear of going to trial, and the advice from other more experienced attorneys helped her overcome her fears.

The mutual support described above is partially attributable to the fact that the Square County Office is staffed only by full-time public defenders. Many of the counties in the state employ part-time public defenders. Alisha described her past experience as a contract attorney for a different county where she did not have the opportunity to learn from and to share legal knowledge with other attorneys to the extent that she now does:

I: I've heard that this office is unique in terms of having full-time public defenders, whereas other counties have only contractors.

A: That's what I first did when I got out of law school. I was in a private practice and contracted for Triangle County, which is about 30 minutes away. But that was *strange* because there was no office to go back and talk to about those cases. I was on my own. Looking back, I wonder how good an attorney I was just right out of law school ... I'm glad I'm here now (personal communication).

Alisha's comments show how past experiences have helped her appreciate how valuable it is to work in an office where attorneys with similar experiences discuss and share ideas.

Helping each other happens naturally in this office, as was illustrated by the attorneys' response to Sally's inexperience when she first arrived. Another factor worth noting is the fact that the office hosts many social events. For example, Richard's birthday fell on the same day as one of Alisha's trial days. When Alisha and I returned to the Public Defender's Office during a recess of the trial, the office was decorated with "Happy 50th Birthday" and "Over the Hill!" signs, and there was a huge cookie to share. A secretary who had helped to decorate the office commented, "[Richard] is one of our favorites." Celebrating Richard's birthday showed that the employees of this office cared about each other. It also provided evidence of the positive working relationship that exists between the secretaries and attorneys in this office.

Jason commented that the workers in the office were like "family," and said, "[In this office, it's] kind of like having a lot of brothers and sisters around you, and they tell you, 'What's going on? Can I help you out?'" (personal communication). When a group of workers operate like a family, individuals are concerned not only with their own well-being, but also for the group as a whole. Sally was cognizant of this fact:

> It's a very knowledgeable office. We've got attorneys in here that just have so much knowledge, so that even though our clients would say, "I don't have an attorney, I have a public defender," in reality, I think there probably isn't more legal knowledge anywhere in the state than in this office. We are just an amazing group of people. (personal communication)

As Sally acknowledges, public defenders do not get much credit for their work. Their clients often view them as "non-attorneys" because they do not have to pay for their services. Yet despite this attitude on the part of their clients (or perhaps because of it), the attorneys worked hard to help and support each other.

4.7.2 Leadership and Autonomy

One might assume that strong leadership would be necessary to help cultivate this kind of culture in an office. However, the manager's style in the Square County Office was supportive rather than directive. When Thom expressed the need for honest relationships with his clients in the previous section, I speculated that one of the reasons that he could be honest with his clients was because he trusted his manager not to fire him just because he had a strong personality and was sometimes brutally honest with his clients. Thom agreed:

> Yes, exactly ... When I was working in a different office, I didn't feel the same protection on me... Paul wants to avoid conflicts, so Paul will come here [Thom's office] and say, "Ashton, don't do that again." And I honestly try not to do it again. But the bottom line is that Paul, he's not going to fire me, you know. I'm here. Yeah, there is a certain security on that, certain safety on that. (personal communication)

The level of comfort and trust that exists between Paul and the attorneys in the office provides a strong foundation for the development of the supportive culture of the office. When asked about this office's low turnover rate, Nick offered two reasons: "[We] like Paul Linton ... We can work somewhere else for more money, but we'd rather work here for less. Basically, we like our boss. Second, freedom, it's flexibility of the schedule" (personal communication).

Nick had worked in different offices in the past, but had sacrificed a better financial situation to be in this office because he preferred to work for Paul. Similarly, Alisha gave up her partnership in a private practice. Nick's comments confirmed the sound relationship existing between the manager and the employees of the Square County Office. Nick also indicated that Paul gave the employees a great deal of freedom. Jason elaborated:

> I feel good in this job. While the pressures are there, the pressures are again self-motivating pressures to do well, to try to do the best you can. As opposed to some external pressure where your boss stands there and says, "Oh, you've got to be in this courtroom, or you've got to do this, you've got to do that." If that were the atmosphere, I probably wouldn't still be here. The atmosphere is one in which I am basically my own boss in a sense, as far as what I do with the cases. Now, if I was screwing up, really not doing a good job, I'm sure somebody would tell me about it, besides the judges, but that's not the case here. (personal communication)

Jason emphasized that in this office the impetus to perform better was internally rather than externally motivated. Each attorney is his or her own boss and is responsible for his or her own work practices. Sally commented on Paul's method of supervising the attorneys in this office:

> ... our evaluation happens almost every day, because if we don't do well, things start to come apart. Luckily all the attorneys here are very competent so that doesn't happen, but I think what you would find is he [Paul] treats us as professionals. So it's almost as if each one of us is expected to be competent, but if there is a problem, he comes right to us, so it's more of a daily thing than yearly thing. (personal communication)

Paul has to accommodate seven unique personalities in one office, but he appeared to be quite successful in keeping the employees happy. Paul gave the attorneys freedom and trusted their expertise. In return, the attorneys worked hard to meet Paul's expectations.

Bob, the office's legal investigator, shared an anecdote about Paul and his old car. Bob knew that Paul spent more money on his aging Volkswagen Rabbit than it was worth. Bob said, "[Paul's old car] aggravates him, it causes him trouble, it doesn't always work. But he still hangs onto it." Bob added, "I'm the same way, too. I aggravate him; I don't always work like I'm supposed to" (personal communication). Bob was using this metaphor to illustrate Paul's willingness to work with idiosyncratic yet competent employees. The importance of a *supportive* manager/supervisor cannot be emphasized enough.

4.7.3 Reality of the Supportive Culture

In addition to the many positive aspects of the Square County Public Defender's Office that we have seen thus far, there were, as one might expect, occasional conflicts between the attorneys. Bob, the office investigator, remarked:

> This office is not without problems. Everything I've told you sounds like it's all honey and lemon, and it's smooth as silk. That's not true. We have differences of opinion, we have serious arguments with other people, but none of it comes away as not having been a learning experience, and that's where your professionalism kicks in. You can yell and scream and pound the table and disagree about the law, or about your opinion of it, and then you just go out to lunch, have lunch together and be friends again. (personal communication)

The attorneys in this office have strong personalities. This sometimes manifests as conflicting opinions on any number of issues. However, by maintaining an awareness of the fact that these conflicts are professional and not personal, the supportive culture of the office persists.

There are also times when the public defenders cannot help each other because of a conflict of interest. For example, when two attorneys are assigned "co-defendants" who have been charged with the same crime, each attorney represents only one defendant and only helps his or her own client. Jason described a situation in which Nick and he each represented defendants involved in the same case:

> First of all, most of what we do is trying to do best for our clients... even in this office, we help each other. We kind of admire each other, but we serve our clients... we are not comfortable because we have a trial where we're defending people who might point fingers and say the other one did [it]. We are standing up there and looking after the interest of our clients. We would be in an essence ... helping a prosecutor because we are fighting each other. (personal communication)

In a case like this, where one defendant says the other committed the crime and vice versa, there is a conflict of interest between the two clients and the attorneys who represent them. This creates a somewhat a tricky situation for the attorneys because they each know other so well. Still, as Jason indicated, these situations come with the territory and do not affect professional relationships.

4.8 Commentary

This chapter was devoted a summary of the important factors that influence the informal learning process in a professional community of practice as illustrated in Fig. 4.1.

Our focus has been on the supportive culture of the office, which is a fundamental component of a successful community of practice. Interviews and observations show that opportunities to learn and a willingness to share information among the attorneys are crucial to the office culture. Interview excerpts illustrate the cooperative nature of the office community. Unlike other counties, which only have contract attorneys, this Public Defender's Office has seven full-time attorneys working in an environment in which they can share and build their knowledge. As Jason pointed out, the office is like a "family," and its members watch out for each other. The tight-knit bond between the attorneys is a core component of the office's community of practice. (see Fig. 4.1 for the concept map).

Sally's comments regarding the clients' attitudes toward the public defenders reveals one of the reasons why this community of practice developed despite the presence of highly individualized work practices (discussed in Section 4.6). Her interview excerpt includes statements about general public perceptions. For example, public defenders are often perceived as inferior to private attorneys because they are obligated to defend the indigent. Public perception of the public defenders, combined with poor chances of winning a majority of cases, creates a measure of adversity that these attorneys must overcome. However, these negative factors actually drive the public defenders to band together – a process that can be perceived as a support mechanism against outside criticism. Barker (1960) argues that undermanned environments foster an individual's commitment to the whole and fosters a feeling of functional self-identity despite the greater insecurity workers may feel in this kind of environment – an argument which supports our understanding of the public defenders' mutual supportiveness. Moreover, a significant factor affecting the culture of the office is the fact that there is no formal competition between the attorneys. The public defenders are hired by the county government, and the office is organized via a flat organizational scheme that contains only two layers: a manager and the rest of the attorneys.

The office's seven independent attorneys have different work styles and personalities. They all have strong opinions about their cases and clients. According to Nick, having a strong personality and holding strong opinions is necessary if one hopes to succeed as a trial attorney. Nick also emphasized the need to have a strong sense of self-worth and faith in one's abilities during a trial in order to persuade jurors that a particular interpretation of the facts surrounding a given case is the correct interpretation.

Finally, observations suggest that the supportive culture of this office derives, at least in part, from Paul's management style. On the surface, the individualized work styles and personalities seem to be competing factors that might undermine a supportive culture. However, Paul has created an environment in which these different personalities help to produce a supportive office culture. As Wenger (1998) points out, "if what makes a community of practice a community is mutual engagement, then it is a kind of community that does not entail homogeneity. Indeed, what makes engagement in practice possible and productive is as much a matter of diversity as it is a matter of homogeneity" (p. 75). The Square County public defenders have unique identities and approaches to their profession. It is their respect for one another, their willingness to offer a helping hand, their common goal, and a manger who leads by example rather than coercion that brings them together.

Chapter 5
Communities of Practice and Information Technologies in the Circle County Public Defender's Office

Up to this point, our focus has been on the Square County public defenders. However, in this chapter, I would like to focus on the role of information technologies in communities of practice. To do this, I will examine another office of public defenders, one that relies heavily on IT to communicate, namely the attorneys in the Circle County Public Defender's Office – home to Shape State's largest metropolis.

Although information technologies sometimes include items other than computers, including overnight delivery (e.g., FedEx), post-it notes, the telephone, voice-mail, fax machines, etc. (Kling, Rosenbaum, & Sawyer, 2005), in this study the discussion of information technologies refers specifically to computer-related technologies that professionals use, including legal databases (e.g., Westlaw, Lexis-Nexis), e-mail, listservs, and the Internet.

Information Technology (IT) research scholars have sought to understand how IT impacts the efficiency of group work. Some researchers focus primarily on time and money as measures of efficiency. For example, IT can connect people in dispersed locations, which has the potential to save money and travel time; however, actual collaboration sometimes does not work well without face-to-face communication (Olson & Olson, 2001). Other researchers have been developing information technologies that improve the effectiveness of teamwork and organizations (e.g., Cohen & Bailey, 1997; DeSanctis & Poole, 1997; Jarvenpaa & Leidner, 1999). As researchers began to recognize the importance of knowledge sharing as a key to fostering learning within organizations, increasing attention has been paid on the effect of IT at workplaces, especially since the late 1990s (Brown & Duguid, 1991, 2000; Wasko & Faraj, 2005). Similarly, the study in this chapter will explore the use of IT to support work practices and to foster professional identities in communities of practice. In addition, a modified social action framework[1] will be proposed based on the analysis.

---

[1] Cf., Ngwenyama and Lyytinen (1997).

N. Hara, *Communities of Practice: Fostering Peer-to-Peer Learning and Informal Knowledge Sharing in the Work Place,* Information Science and Knowledge Management 13, © Springer-Verlag Berlin Heidelberg 2009

5.1 Site Description

The public defender's office in Circle County is the largest public defender's office in the state, and at the time of the study, employed 57 full-time attorneys, 50–60 part-time contract attorneys, and 35–40 full-time support staff. Due to an increasing case load, the Circle County had blossomed in size during the 5 years leading up to the current study.

The county has a massive court system (20 courts including misdemeanor courts, Class D felony courts, major felony courts, a drug court, a drug treatment court, a major case unit, which specializes in murder and death penalty cases, and various juvenile courts). As such, the attorneys' roles are more specialized than the ones in Square County. Each attorney is assigned to one court, and there is also a higher degree of specialization (i.e., each attorney handles only major felony cases, murder and death penalty cases, Class D felony cases, misdemeanor cases, or juvenile cases). Young attorneys, who generally do not have much experience, usually start in a court that handles misdemeanors. A contract attorney who had been working for this office explained to me how the system of promotion works:

> ...most of the new attorneys will start at the misdemeanor position if they don't have any experience... or they will go to juvenile... And it's learning by fire because you are thrown in, and you are given hundreds of cases, and you are told to go handle them. It's like a fraternity; everybody has to do it before you can get to do the felony. (personal communication)

After they have more experience, attorneys may move up to a Class D felony court and eventually a major felony court. This is the ladder of promotion for public defenders in this office.

Despite the office size, the attorneys still have caseloads as heavy as those working in the Square County Public Defender's Office. According to Circle County's chief public defender, a full-time attorney in a major felony court has approximately 100 assignments in a year; however, an attorney who is assigned to more time consuming cases, like death penalty cases, generally handles no more than one at a time, although there are always exceptions. Class D felony attorneys, on the other hand, have 100–150 open cases at a time, whereas the attorneys in misdemeanor court handle 1,500–2,000 cases annually. Juvenile-case attorneys, who are not included in the study, handled about 800 cases each in the previous year. Because of the heavy caseloads, misdemeanor/D felony attorneys are often unable to meet all their clients before their first court date.

Compared to the office in Square County, the office in Circle County witnesses a rapid turnover rate. Attorneys come and go at a brisk pace. During my observations and interviews at the office, I encountered quite a few "going-away" parties. Rhonda Smith, the supervisor of the misdemeanor/D felony division confirmed my observation, and she described the difficulty of keeping the people she had assigned to the misdemeanor/D felony courts:

> Our turnover is so high here – people are either getting promoted or leaving for another job... They come in misdemeanor court, and hopefully they would be there for at least 6 months, but sometimes they are in misdemeanor court for maybe 2 months. Then they go

to D felony or domestic violence court. Then, they stay there for a little while and Alex [the supervisor for the major felony courts] comes. When Alex has openings, the first place he comes in and looks is my courts. If he takes people out of my D felony courts, I have to move more misdemeanor people up and hire brand-new people into misdemeanors. (personal communication)

Although promotion is generally considered to be good news, it is bad news for Rhonda. She estimated that on the average, one person quits or leaves every month. As Rhonda noted, "Every single year, I lose about 12 people." She supervises 23 attorneys, which means that she loses and replaces roughly half of the attorneys every year. According to her, the reasons they leave are twofold: the first is because they are promoted to the major felony courts; the second is that some move to private practice where the pay is better.

5.2 IT as Support for Practice in the Circle County Public Defender's Office

The IT infrastructure in the Circle County Public Defender's Office is much more sophisticated than in other public defender's offices in the state. Since 1995 or 1996, every attorney has had an office computer. At the time of the study, the office had a regular e-mail system, called GroupWise, and Internet access. The attorneys also had access to a listserv that connected them to other defense attorneys in the state. Each computer was hooked up to a Local Area Network (LAN), so that the attorneys had access to databases for criminal records and police reports available in Circle County. They also have access to legal-research tools, such as LexisNexis and Premise, a product of Westlaw.

Information technology played several roles in support of legal practice in this Public Defender's Office. The organization did not have a master plan for using IT to connect these public defenders, but observations were made to examine the way in which IT was used. In this chapter, the framework developed by Ngwenyama and Lyytinen (1997) is used to categorize the roles played by IT in the Circle County Public Defender's Office. Ngwenyama and Lyytinen propose the following four categories of social action supported by groupware: instrumental, communicative, discursive, and strategic.

Instrumental action is examined within the context of the means by which IT helps to achieve end results by controlling, manipulating, and transforming physical artifacts, such as case documents. As Elliott and Kling (1997) indicate, the use of computerized legal-research tools has been frequently observed among legal professionals. Examples of instrumental action include the attorneys' use of IT for legal research (e.g., searching the Internet, LexisNexis, and Premise); database research (e.g., searching the Patio system, which contains criminal records, court procedures, and police reports); and knowledge sharing (e.g., contributing to and searching a shared directory) in order to support legal work practices.

The creation and maintenance of shared understanding among members who are engaged in accomplishing the same goal is indicative of communicative action. Within our understanding of communicative action, two major categories exist: one-to-one personal communication, and news/information sharing. Example technologies that facilitate communicative action include e-mail and computer conferencing. For communicative action, e-mail is a primary tool used by the public defenders in the Circle County Office.

Discursive action refers to "the specification and evaluation of goals, objectives, and action-plans, and the achieving of a rational consensus on values and norms that will guide collaborative action" (Ngwenyama & Lyytinen, 1997, p. 77). In the Circle County Public Defender's Office, discussion mainly took place on the e-mail list (PD-l) provided by the Shape State Public Defender Council. Approximately 250 defense attorneys statewide subscribed to PD-l. Roughly 20 percent of the attorneys in the Circle County Public Defender's Office were subscribers. In interviews, these attorneys reported using PD-l in a number of different ways: to ask questions; share updates about statutes, judges, and prosecutors; brainstorm strategies; discuss current legal issues; and learn from each other. Thus, while personal e-mails often were used for communicative actions in this office, discussions via PD-l were discursive and accessible to all participants.

Working with individuals to systematically achieve certain goals is the end result of strategic action. It often involves negotiation and bargaining. For example, public defenders used strategic action when they used e-mail to negotiate plea agreements with prosecutors.

Table 5.1 summarizes IT use in the Circle County Public Defender's Office based on each of Ngwenyama and Lyytinen's (1997) categories. The social action categories were further divided into smaller ones called "supported work."

Table 5.1 Roles of IT in the public defender's office in Circle County (adapted from Ngwenyama & Lyytinen (1997)

Social Action	Supported Work	Software/Tool
Instrumental	Legal research	LexisNexis, Premise, Internet
	Evidence collection	Patio (criminal records & police reports)
	Knowledge sharing	Shared directory
Communicative	One-to-one, one-to-many communications	e-mail
	News/Information sharing	e-mail
Discursive	Discussion	Pubdef-L (listserv)
Strategic	Negotiation w/prosecutors	e-mail

Patio and Pubdef-L are pseudonyms.

5.2.1 Differences between Younger Attorneys and Experienced Attorneys

As one might expect, observations in Circle County found that less-experienced attorneys were likely to be more comfortable using computers and communicating online, whereas experienced attorneys tended to rely more on talking to people, especially their colleagues. Conversely, more-experienced attorneys seemed to believe that face-to-face interactions were more important and necessary than electronic communication. However, it should be noted that e-mail was an important IT tool supporting communicative action for *everyone* in the office. The older, more experienced attorneys' IT usage varied from the younger attorneys' *except* for the use of e-mail. Elizabeth Fox, a major felony attorney, admitted the value of it, and said, "I could not get by without the e-mail. I don't remember what it was like not to have it. We rely on it so much." On the other hand, major felony attorneys use e-mail less for certain types of interactions, like brainstorming with other office attorneys. Elizabeth said, "It would take so long to write it all down. It's easier to go say, 'Hey, look, you got ten minutes, let me bounce this off of you, what do you think?' Much quicker than writing" (personal communication). When brainstorming with colleagues, these attorneys valued prompt feedback. In a similar way, Joanne Kent, a major felony attorney, explained the difference between e-mail and face-to-face communication:

> The one thing with e-mail is you have to make a concerted effort to do it. When we were together in one building, you are walking down the hall and overhear a conversation... you might hear something interesting that you might want to listen to or you might have had the case like that a month before or a year before, and you just enter the conversation, "oh, oh, oh, I had a case like that. And this is what we did." Or "what are you gonna do because I couldn't figure out how to do that?" So, you have all spontaneous wonderful conversations. E-mail is different... Gina Dean who used to be next door. We used to talk all the time. But oddly enough [because of] the division of the floor, we don't anymore. And we don't talk much with e-mail... It's not a substitute. (personal communication)

The above comment implies that e-mail might be useful for distributing and exchanging information, but might not be appropriate for brainstorming and more involved conversations.

In the following example a combination of instrumental and communicative actions are facilitated by IT use. Given the budgetary resources of the Circle County Office, a database ("Patio") has been developed for the criminal justice system. Use of Patio had become embedded in the attorneys' work practices. An important point to keep in mind is that the attorneys in this office are not necessarily assigned to the same clients when the clients are charged with new offenses. Sometimes a person has cases in two or three different courts with various attorneys, and those attorneys are not always informed about their client's other cases. To compensate for this, the attorneys use Patio to search criminal records to find out whether other attorneys are representing the same clients.

Another way IT is used for instrumental action among the Circle County attorneys is via a shared electronic directory in the office, which contains every attorney's pleadings and motions so that other attorneys can refer to such documents and use similar filings for different cases. Several attorneys mentioned that this directory was a useful tool, although it seemed to be used more frequently by less experienced attorneys. Ann Howard, a young attorney said:

> You can go in there [the shared directory], and there are lots of motions that everybody in the office has used at one point in time or standard motions. And you just go in and change names and case number. So, you don't have to do a whole new motion. I use that a lot... It's very handy. (personal communication)

Other attorneys mentioned that they did not use the shared directory because they wanted to develop their own documents. Major felony attorneys mentioned that although they formerly used the shared directory, most had developed their own collection of legal motions over the years. As such, the shared directory seemed less pertinent to them. There was some concern that the less experienced attorneys might be tempted to focus solely on the use of easily available documents without giving serious consideration to the suitability of the material. The easy availability of these shared documents might result in filings that are not well-crafted (i.e., filings that overlook less accessible but more relevant materials). In such a scenario, IT use in instrumental action can be a double-edged sword, saving much-needed time but jeopardizing the quality of the output.

Another IT resource used in this office, the e-mail list PD-l, falls under the category of discursive action. To give an idea of the content shared on PD-l, Cathy Bruce, a misdemeanor attorney, shared an example of the discussions on PD-l:

> ...here is an attorney who is asking everybody on PD-l... if anybody is out there who knows anything about this issue that he has, and what would they do. And he has a bunch of responses already... So anybody who knows anything about it will respond. If you put a message on, it goes to the entire group. That's like information sharing we have on a computer, and not everyone in this office is a member of it. It's an excellent resource. (personal communication)

Cathy's comments provide insight into practical applications of PD-l and indicate that an attorney who posts a question usually receives many responses in a short amount of time. She valued PD-l as an information resource as well as a means for collaborative brainstorming. On the other hand, Alex Gordon, the supervisor of the major felony attorneys, warned that attorneys needed to be selective about the information obtained through PD-l by saying there was "lots of junk in it" (personal communication). Therefore, it is necessary for attorneys who read PD-l discussions to evaluate the quality of the information obtained.

Despite the limitations of these IT resources, attorneys who work in the Misdemeanor/D felony division are inclined to integrate IT into their work practices to support instrumental, communicative, and discursive actions.

5.3 Younger Attorneys, Communities of Practice, and IT Support of Identity Formation

Communities of practice have two major axes – practice and identity (Wenger, 1998). The profession or practice of a group of workers is obviously a core component of a community of practice because, as the name suggests, a community of practice forms around a certain practice, such as legal practice, medical practice, teaching practice, etc. However, the identity component is not as intuitive. If we accept that practice is a fundamental component of a community of practice, the next step is to understand how identity serves as the glue that connects members of the community. Identity in this context is the underlying philosophy that serves to attract and retain the members of a community. Contrary to expectations, identity formation did not appear to be strongly supported by information technology. In the following section, attorneys new to the profession are the focal point of our discussion because they are in the early, formative stages of developing their professional identities.

5.3.1 Younger Attorneys in Communities of Practice

There exist several different communities of practice within the Circle County Public Defender's Office. The office grew into a large organization between the mid- and late-1990s, during which time the practicalities of improving the expertise of younger public defenders became increasingly vital to the organization. Due to a lack of office space, the attorneys in the office work in three locations: the less experienced attorneys work in the main office, the more experienced attorneys work in an office one block away, and the juvenile-case attorneys are located in the juvenile justice center.[2] The physical separation of the first two groups means that less experienced attorneys have fewer interactions with more experienced attorneys. The training director expressed some concern about this issue:

> We've grown so much. We used to all be in this building, and about a year ago we were practically sitting on each other's laps. We were really too crowded, and we had to rent space about a block away. The major felony attorneys are now down there, which is unfortunate because what we have here are the younger attorneys. And they share information among themselves, and that's great and good. But, they don't get that opportunity very much to have that informal learning with those [more experienced] attorneys anymore because they are far away. (personal communication)

As a result of physical separation, one community of practice developed among more experienced attorneys dealing with major felony cases. These public defenders share a strong sense of professionalism and are mutually supportive of each other. Other communities of practice developed among the less experienced attorneys who handled less serious offenses, such as misdemeanor and Class D felony cases. Ties

---

[2] This last division was not included in the study.

between members of the latter groups (misdemeanor/D felony attorneys) do not seem as strong as those between the more experienced attorneys.

During interviews, both the less experienced and more experienced attorneys mentioned the lack of interaction between the two groups. Linda Ellis, a misdemeanor attorney, explained why she did not interact frequently with the major felony attorneys. The first reason was, "I don't talk to major felony attorneys primarily because they are not here." The second reason was lack of time, and the third was because the other group had different issues from hers as a misdemeanor attorney:

> Most of the time when you need to solve problems or get information, you are kind of in a time crunch, so you don't necessarily have time to go over there to see who is available. Also the issues sometimes are normally limited to misdemeanor court, while the major felony attorneys are more familiar with A, B, and C felonies. (personal communication)

The fact that different legal issues are handled by the misdemeanor/D felony and the major felony courts came up repeatedly when I talked with misdemeanor/D felony attorneys. Because they handle different types of cases than those in the major felony courts, the misdemeanor attorneys insisted that the legal issues they handled were significantly different.

The major felony attorneys had a different perspective on the lack of interaction. Roy Stewart, a major felony attorney, was aware of the importance of the interaction between the two groups, but mentioned that the reality was that there were, in fact, very few interactions.

Mike Taylor, the chief public defender, looked back on his decision to move half of the office to the new location:

> I didn't realize how devastating that would be to this experience sharing, knowledge sharing, and office camaraderie and so forth until I actually experienced it. Being a half block up the street doesn't seem like it's that bad of a deal. But the fact of the matter is, if I have a major felony lawyer there, and I've got a misdemeanor/D felony lawyer who has a question, they have to go either "I've gotta make time to walk half a block up the street," or "I have to hope that I see him," instead of walking by the person's office and having an interchange... Also, you develop personal relationships with these people, and there becomes a natural mentoring that goes on... Boy, I'd be very sensitive to that in the future. (personal communication)

Mike states that he did not foresee the extent to which the interaction might be reduced when he made the decision to move half of the office. Both Mike and Roy express concerns about the lack of interaction between the experienced and less experienced attorneys. However, Linda, one of the less experienced attorneys, did not give much thought to the lack of opportunities she had to interact with major felony attorneys. I also noted this during my interviews with the other misdemeanor/D felony attorneys. Although they were somewhat aware of the fact that it would have been nice to have had opportunities to discuss their issues and questions, they seemed to be overwhelmed by the volume of the cases and could not think beyond the cases they were dealing with at that moment. Moreover, the attorneys interviewed in misdemeanor/D felony courts had been working for the office less than a year, and thus had not experienced dialogues with the more experienced attorneys. Because the misdemeanor/D felony attorneys had never experienced this, they could not be fully aware of what they were missing.

Although the office has tried to overcome the sense of isolation felt by some of the less experienced attorneys, the invisible social line between these groups has not disappeared; indeed, the training director indicated that she felt that the sense of separation was growing even stronger. For example, the training director introduced two gatherings in an attempt to integrate the groups: a regular lunch meeting and a mentoring program. No incentive was offered to support these programs; instead, participation relied on each attorney being self-motivated enough to seek opportunities for professional development. However, all the attorneys interviewed mentioned having difficulty with this "forced socialization." This type of top-down initiative to improve information sharing is often unsuccessful (George, Iacono, & Kling, 1995). Additionally, the lack of appropriate incentives may have contributed to low participation (cf., Orlikowski, 1996).

Although one would expect to find different communities of practice in almost any professional group, an unusually strong dichotomy exists in the Circle County Public Defender's Office between less experienced and more experienced attorneys (see Fig. 5.1). Misdemeanor/D felony attorneys have their own separate community of practice, which is further segmented. As shown in Fig. 5.1, communities of practice among the less experienced attorneys (mainly in the Misdemeanor/D felony division) tend to develop based on which court the attorneys regularly work. Consequently, the communities of practice among less experienced attorneys may not be as strong as the single community that exists among the major felony attorneys.

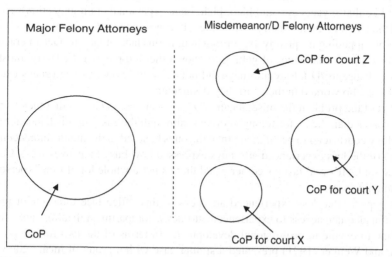

Fig. 5.1 Illustration of communities of practice distribution in the Circle County Public Defender's Office

5.3.2 *Isolation, Overload, and Work Specialization*

It was speculated that the isolation of less experienced attorneys created a situation in which they would be forced to rely more on the Internet, internal e-mail, and the e-mail list than on learning directly from experienced attorneys. For example, Julie, a D felony attorney, said:

> I don't talk to major felony attorneys. Primarily because they are not here, so I don't have their availability as much... Certainly I do talk to people at [the major felony division], but it's normally by phone just because physically we are not usually in the same spot.

Harry Johnson, a D felony attorney, pointed out problems with a lack of direct face-to-face – or at least verbal – communication among the attorneys in general. First, he explained that e-mail does not facilitate interacting much with others:

> E-mail is easy to communicate obviously because if you know somebody's address, you just send them out. The hard part is .... Like I've done a certain amount of research on certain issues, but nobody would know that unless they talked to me face-to-face. They could e-mail me and say, "What do you have?" And they won't do that just randomly, set up the system randomly and e-mail me every week to see if I know something new. So, you have to know where the information is, and that's not so good right now.

His comments illustrate the need for attorneys to understand the specific expertise of their colleagues before even asking questions. However, when asked if he had regular opportunities to speak to experienced attorneys face-to-face, he responded, "No. Outside of my court I don't. [I can't] just grab somebody from major felony, and chit chat, and talk about all my cases and he might know, 'Oh, yeah, I had an issue like that 6 years ago and blah, blah, blah'" (personal communication). Harry rued the fact that the interaction with other attorneys in the office, even face-to-face, was not happening frequently. According to him, this lack of face-to-face interaction is rooted in the challenges of getting to know other attorneys. Like Harry, most of the misdemeanor/D felony attorneys did not seem to know other attorneys except for those who worked in the court they frequented.

Part of the problem the misdemeanor/D felony attorneys have is that they handle more cases than the major felony attorneys, although the cases in misdemeanor and D felony courts tend to be "lighter" than the ones handled in the major felony courts. Many of the less experienced attorneys expressed how busy their lives were. Cathy Bruce said, "It's real fast paced here, and there's not a whole lot of time" (personal communication).

It appears that less experienced attorneys in this office face three major problems: inadequate access to experienced attorneys, compartmentalization, and a lack of time to devote to professional development. In terms of the two former points, Lave and Wenger (1991) presented a similar case with a group of meat cutters. In order to increase work efficiency, the apprentice butchers worked in a separate place where they were not able to observe journeymen, but instead were assigned minor tasks. Marshall states that "the physical layout of a work setting is an important dimension of learning, since apprentices get a great deal from observing others and being observed" (cited in Lave & Wenger, 1991, p. 78). He also argues that specialization of tasks (i.e., compartmentalization), is not beneficial for either apprentices or journeymen because it limits the ability of workers to learn the full range of tasks.

The Public Defender's Office in Circle County faces a similar situation. When I observed the routine of one D felony attorney, I realized that the attorney had few opportunities to observe more experienced attorneys. This was because he had been assigned to a D felony court where all the cases were of the same type, and all of the attorneys had a similar level of expertise. In other words, the younger attorneys were not given "legitimate peripheral participation" opportunities (Lave & Wenger, 1991). Because of the lack of interaction with more experienced attorneys, misdemeanor/D felony attorneys did not have many chances to learn what it is like to be a public defender and to develop their professional identity.

Likewise, the attorneys' work specialization has created an environment where less experienced attorneys practice without observing more experienced attorneys and without having the opportunity to learn from them. Similarly, Nonaka and Takeuchi (1995) also emphasize the importance of overlapping work. While work overlaps tend to be perceived as a waste and are avoided in the pursuit of efficiency in Western companies, the existence of a certain level of work overlap also creates an environment where employees can learn from each other. The separate locations of the Circle County Public Defender's Offices create a situation in which less experienced attorneys do not naturally socialize with more experienced attorneys.

In Vaughan's study (1997), engineers working on the Challenger spacecraft were overscheduled and did not have time to reflect on their work, a fact that may have compounded factors leading to the 1986 disaster. Although misdemeanor/D felony attorneys are encouraged to observe major felony attorneys' trials,[3] the overwhelming number of cases they have to handle makes this very difficult. A major attorney commented:

> I know they are busy, too. I've done these courts .... There are a couple [of attorneys] who are good about it, but for the most part, I get the impression that they don't care, or they know everything. I might be wrong. But that's the impression I got.

Only a few less experienced public defenders sit through major felony trials. While misdemeanor/D felony attorneys mentioned that they do not have the time to sit through 3-day trials because they already have assigned court days, major felony attorneys expressed disappointment about these younger attorneys' lack of engagement. The compensation for these less experienced attorneys is salary-based, and therefore, given their existing caseload, these attorneys have little incentive to attend additional court cases.

---

[3] Everyone's trial schedules are announced in advance. Major felony attorneys mentioned that observing more experienced attorneys' trials is one of the best ways to learn.

5.3.3 Professional Identity among Younger Attorneys

In the public defender's offices, attorneys often learn about their profession by socializing with other attorneys. Attorneys' attitudes toward their profession – that of public defender – differ between the two groups. The major felony attorneys appear to be more dedicated to being public defenders, whereas the majority of the less experienced attorneys are more likely to describe their jobs as "a way to get more experience." Socialization only seems to occur among those who are physically located in the same office.

It is unfortunate that the interactions between these two groups occurs so infrequently because this means that each group's knowledge is confined to the members of the legal group and is rarely shared between the attorneys at the two locations. The younger attorneys are not the only ones to suffer as a result of the situation. Elizabeth Fox, a major felony attorney, recalled an incident when she had benefited greatly from an interaction with less experienced attorneys:

> I had this jury trial . . . last week. . . And these two guys from the other building just happened to wander over here. . . And we just talked through it like for an hour, and I totally had my argument all made up. It was great, and I won the hearing the next day because those guys came over here. And they were junior lawyers. They were incredibly helpful. . . I think that they should try to get involved in more. (personal communication)

This is likely a somewhat uncommon scenario. Usually experienced attorneys help out the less experienced ones, not the other way around. This anecdote should prove encouraging for the less experienced attorneys, as it bears witness to the fact that they are not the only ones to benefit from interactions with their more experienced colleagues.

Elizabeth has firsthand knowledge of the demanding situation in the misdemeanor/D felony courts; she used to work there before being moved up to handle major felony cases. However, she stated that the misdemeanor/D felony attorneys do not take advantage of the educational experiences available them, such as the monthly lunch meetings, the mentoring program, and opportunities to help major felony attorneys with jury trials. Elizabeth mentioned another situation in which the misdemeanor/D felony attorneys do not participate:

> We will tell Nancy [the training director] when we have a jury trial, and then she will try to find one of them to sit with us so they can sit through a jury trial, and no one volunteers to sit with us. I know they have a lot to do, but you can learn a lot from watching. So, they are going to a jury trial without ever having done one or at least having seen one. It makes no sense. (personal communication)

Elizabeth's comments underscore the valuable learning opportunities available to younger public defenders. While misdemeanor/D felony attorneys might not see observing major felony cases as a learning opportunity because these cases may not have direct connections to their own, these experiences actually have the potential to be of real use.

The Circle County public defenders who work on misdemeanor/D felony cases seem to have a lack of professional commitment. This may stem from a scarcity of chances to interact with the senior attorneys who have developed professional identities, from being new to the profession, and also from the less challenging work assignments that they have as junior public defenders.

5.3.4 Younger Attorneys' Heavy Reliance on IT

There are a number of factors that affect the development of the public defenders' professional identity. However, the tendency to rely too much on electronic communication media in the early stages of their careers has the potential to impede whether and when they form professional identities because this type of knowledge is difficult to transmit in electronic environments. I found that less experienced attorneys tended to rely more on knowledge that exists outside the office rather than on the know-how of colleagues, perhaps because of their physical isolation. For example, David said:

> There's no training session right now for D felony attorneys because you have your mentor, but like me and Nancy, there's no chance to talk because she is too busy. So pretty much [you] just ought to learn on your own, get everything done, that's where GroupWise, PD-1 and the Internet come into play. Because I can just stay at this place, and it doesn't take much time to pull it. I just bookmark every page and pull it out to see what came down today. I can check everything in a half hour. (personal communication)

Even though relying on electronic resources sounds like a wonderful solution, it is doubtful that less experienced attorneys can obtain a sense of professional identity via these remote electronic formats.

To better understand this, consider the use of the PD-1 e-mail list. Pubdef-L provides information about laws, current issues in the field, feedback, and brainstorming opportunities, but it does not seem to support the formation of professional identities among misdemeanor/D felony attorneys. The same thing could be said more broadly of all computer-mediated communication (CMC) methods used in this office; they do not appear to support professional identity formation among less experienced attorneys. Research on CMC in education has shown that the students who use online conferencing tools tend to be too task specific and less social than those who use face-to-face communication (Cooney, 1998). The content of the e-mail list is static, often lacks crucial real-world context, and does not provide robust opportunities for less experienced attorneys to learn (e.g., face-to-face interaction with more experienced attorneys).

In addition, attorneys do not use CMC to discuss what went wrong in lost trials, how public defenders can improve their practice, or how to respond when people ask them why they decided to become public defenders despite the low status of the public defender profession. On the other hand, these types of discussions do occur during face-to-face communication. In a sense, less experienced attorneys are missing out on crucial conversations that have the potential to make them better attorneys when they rely too heavily on CMC for professional development.

5.4 IT Supports Practice, but Not Identity Formation

At the risk of sounding like an optimist, I would like to point out that there are some IT applications that significantly support Circle County public defenders' work practices. Almost all the attorneys in the public defender's office frequently use IT to support instrumental action (such as LexisNexis for research), as well as using IT for communicative action (e.g., e-mail) and for discursive action (e.g., list-servs).

I also found that misdemeanor/D felony attorneys tend to use all IT applications more frequently than do major felony attorneys. There appear to be two reasons for this. The first reason is that misdemeanor/D felony attorneys are younger, and as one might expect, more comfortable using IT. Second, they are relatively isolated, and as such, do not have access to knowledgeable human resources like the more experienced attorneys do. Other studies of teachers (Selwyn, 2000) and mathematicians (Walsh & Bayma, 1996) have found that electronic communication can help reduce isolation among those who tend to be separated physically from their peers.

Personally, I do not think the four social actions proposed by Ngwenyama and Lyytinen (1997) sufficiently describe how IT supports communities of practice. Therefore, I propose expanding the framework to include another category called "development of professional identity" (see Table 5.2). All the social actions in Ngwenyama and Lyytinen are categorized as practice, yet a major component of communities of practice is missing from the picture. The proposed framework shown in Table 5.2 accommodates both practice *and* identity. Rhetorical action refers to a means of perpetuating the raison d'être of the profession. For example, one of the questions asked most frequently of public defenders is why they chose

Table 5.2 Proposed roles of IT in the Public Defender's Office in Circle County (modified from Wenger, 1998; and Ngwenyama & Lyytinen, 1997)

CoP Framework	Social Action	Supported Work	Software/Tool
Practice	Instrumental	Legal research tool	LexisNexis, Premise, Internet
		Evidence collection	Patio (criminal records & police reports)
		Knowledge sharing	Shared directory
	Communicative	One-to-one, one-to-many communication	e-mail
		News/Information sharing	e-mail
	Discursive	Discussion	Pubdef-L (listserv)
	Strategic	Negotiation w/prosecutors	e-mail
Identity	Rhetorical	Development of professional identity	Face-to-face discussions
			Videoconferencing
			Instant messaging

the profession. Roy Stewart, a major felony attorney, explained why he decided to become a public defender and used the term "underdogs" to describe his situation:

> I've never had a desire to do anything else. My whole idea about going to law school is that I wanted to be a trial lawyer, and what I enjoy doing is jury trials. Most lawyers don't see the inside of the courtroom; they don't practice in court, but I've always wanted to do that. I guess personally my inclinations have always been to fight for the underdog. It just feels important that peoples' rights, [that] there's somebody to fight for those rights and the constitution. (personal communication)

This is an example of rhetoric used by the more experienced public defenders when discussing the profession.

(Un)fortunately, it is very difficult to facilitate this rhetorical action with IT, despite some authors' assertions (e.g., Hildreth, 2004; Huber, 1996; Huseman & Goodman, 1999; Sharp, 1997; Wenger, 2001) that IT can foster organizational learning and/or communities of practice. No support for such a claim was observed in the Circle County Public Defender's Office environment. Gottschalk (1999), who conducted a survey of Norwegian law firms and their use of IT for knowledge management, also found that there is no correlation between cooperative culture and IT use for knowledge management. In the current study, less experienced attorneys exhibited a marked penchant for use of IT for social actions, and as a result, formed relatively weak and segmented communities of practice. Conversely, the major felony attorneys used less IT for instrumental and strategic actions and some IT for communicative and discursive actions. They had a strong community of practice. Thus, high IT use does not automatically lead to a strong community of practice.

In fact, these findings lead me to speculate that heavy reliance on IT for communicative action at early stages of a career may actually lessen the participation in communities of practice, as is the case with many of the less experienced attorneys in Circle County. In fact, high use of IT may create the illusion that IT helps these public defenders to advance their careers, but it did not seem to help younger attorneys I observed in the development of their professional identities, which is crucial to their professional development. Less experienced attorneys tend to overlook the importance of professional socialization, which naturally emerges from informal interactions between new and more experienced colleagues. Van Maanen (1973), who observed policemen, found that it was vital for new police officers to learn to become a part of their professional community through apprenticeship and informal interactions. Likewise, major felony attorneys in Circle County have incorporated socialization in their daily practices through their preference for face-to-face communications.

5.5 Commentary

In this chapter, I have illustrated different types of communities of practice and the role of IT in supporting work practices and identity formation within the communities. The community of practice that exists among experienced attorneys is made manifest in the presence of a sense of professionalism and mutual support, whereas the communities of practice among less experienced attorneys appeared to be fragmented and limited to those who worked in the same courts. While these latter communities of practice resemble the community of practice formed by the major felony attorneys in character, their ties to the larger community appear to be weaker than that of the major felony attorneys. There seem to be different factors that make the less experienced attorneys' community of practice more tenuous: (1) they do not have immediate access to experienced attorneys (location); (2) they are overwhelmed by the number of cases they handle (overload); (3) the specialization of their tasks creates segregation and often does not allow them to observe more experienced attorneys who handle different types of cases; and (4) they are younger lawyers with limited experience.

Interviews and observations reveal that the public defenders in this office use IT to support all of Ngwenyama and Lyytinen's (1997) four social actions except "strategic" (see Table 5.1). Hence, IT in this office plays a major role in supporting attorneys' work practices and in connecting the attorneys to each other. On the other hand, IT does not seem to help bridge the gap between the two groups of public defenders. A modification of Ngwenyama and Lyytinen (1997)'s model is proposed to provide support for the development of professional identity in communities of practice that rely heavily on IT (see Table 5.2). More studies need to be done to empirically examine and validate the proposed framework.

This chapter also questions some of the claims made concerning the ability of IT to cultivate communities of practice. The chapter started by discussing efficiency and effectiveness with IT. The use of IT may help less experienced attorneys to become more efficient, but this does not mean that using IT is effective in helping to develop professional identity. The concept of communities of practice is rich and complex, and this study has revealed that high IT use does not necessarily produce a strong community of practice. I speculate that heavy reliance on IT use for communicative action may even weaken ties within a community.

Although these findings emerged from a case study of public defenders, I believe that this ethnographic study also sheds light on the role of communities of practice and IT in other professions. In the next chapter, the discussion will focus on communities of practice that exist entirely online.

Chapter 6
Online Communities of Practice: Beyond Organizational Boundaries

It is becoming increasing common for organizations and professional associations to examine the potential of online communication networks to enable members to share knowledge and engage in continuing workplace learning and professional development (Gray, 2004; Wasko & Faraj, 2005). Holding face-to-face interactions on a regular basis can be costly and time consuming, and online communities of practice supported by Internet technologies are among the few viable alternatives to live conversation and knowledge sharing (Ardichvili, Page, & Wentling, 2003; Dubé, Bourhis, & Jacob, 2005). However, little documented research categorizes the different types of knowledge that workers share with one another in online environments. Recently, several studies have addressed knowledge sharing. For example, Wasko and Faraj (2000) examined why people contribute to the provision of knowledge as a public good in online communities of practice, although they stopped short of investigating the types of knowledge that were shared. A similar trend was noted in other studies (e.g., Ardichvili et al., 2003; Hendriks, 1999). More importantly, previous studies have not addressed the types of knowledge or factors that can help sustain knowledge sharing in online communities.

This chapter will first examine the nature of a listserv that helped to foster an online community of practice among public defenders in one state. I will then consider the nature of online discussions, the extension of communication on the listserv to face-to-face discourse, and some drawbacks of the listserv.

6.1 Online Community of Practice among Public Defenders

Pubdef-L is supported by the Shape State Public Defender Council to assist defense attorneys. Listserv membership consisted of approximately 250 attorneys at the time of the study. This listserv is not open to the public. In order to be a part of PD-l, a user must be a member of the State Public Defender Council and send in a formal request to join the listserv. The traffic on PD-l is relatively heavy; there were 214 messages within two randomly chosen weeks. Linda Ellis, a misdemeanor attorney who subscribes to PD-l, summarized its characteristics in the following manner: "There are a lot of experienced lawyers on there, so you get different information. A lot of wisdom comes through PD-l to help problem solve and give suggestions, cite cases, find cases. It's a good asset" (personal communication). Roy Stewart, a major felony attorney, also had high regard for PD-l:

> It's not uncommon for an attorney in a small county to ask a question, "How do I deal with the situation?" and he'll get responses. Other defense attorneys are willing to help. The attorneys in [places] all over the state give him some ideas. So, that's really helpful. That's like being able to brainstorm with your whole community of defense attorneys... It's all come about within the last three or four years. Before that, I don't know how people kept them in touch. (personal communication)

Despite already possessing considerable knowledge and experience, Roy valued the information coming through PD-l because he considered it a brainstorming tool for those within the community of defense attorneys. It can also be inferred that PD-l helps connect the defense attorneys throughout the state and helps to create a sense of a community among them.

As described in Section 5.2.1 of Chapter 5, a number of questions and answers, as well as information exchange occur on PD-l. David Steven, a D felony attorney, provided an example of discussions on PD-l:

> For example, if an attorney has a case that he is working on, we'll talk about the case [through] e-mail. He'll send out the facts of the case, and then what happens: Why did the cop pull the person over? Is this a valid stop? Is there any reason I could suppress everything if it's not a valid stop? And then everyone will respond, if it is or isn't a valid stop, you can ask the cop these questions. Sometimes officers pull somebody over before they have a reason to stop them. If they pull them over too soon, then it's an invalid stop. There is always an issue like that. People want to ask questions. It's a pretty broad range of issues that come up... There's a lot of stuff that comes up that I've never seen before. So I can read the question and responses and learn from that.

David's description provides a concrete idea of the typical discussions on PD-l – asking for feedback and opinions about a current case. As Roy mentioned previously, PD-l serves as a brainstorming forum for attorneys because everyone responds to the entire list, not just to the person who raised the question.

Pickering and King (1995) examined the motivation of the use of e-mail in interorganization communication. They noted that "most of the messages posted to Usenet newsgroups are requests for particular information and assistance with problem-solving" (p. 481); the discussions on PD-l have similar characteristics. Pickering and King further argued that interorganizational computer-mediated communication (CMC) supports dispersed occupational communities. Pubdef-L appears to uphold this function as well.

In addition to information sharing and problem solving, there is another function of PD-l. Cathy Bruce, a misdemeanor attorney, stated that PD-l was a great learning resource as well:

> Since I'm new, I just learn a lot. I'm not at a point where [I'm responding much]...maybe once I've responded. But I just learn a lot from hearing about different issues. And I've started to create research folders. And I don't respond as much

because I don't know a whole lot about what they are asking. (personal communication)

Hence, PD-1 provides a learning space for both less experienced and more experienced attorneys. Joanne Kent, a major felony attorney, added:

Pubdef-L is a statewide defense network. I don't know how many messages I read every day, probably dozens. So you have a lot of attorneys that you are talking to… It's the same thing as leaning on everybody's door because people will throw out a fact pattern, and people all over the state will respond. And say, "Oh, yeah, I've heard about the case down in Rectangle County, and they did such and such. The prosecutor's approach was this way, or the judge said this or that. That sentence was done in this way." It's like… walking past and overhearing conversation and joining in. That's neat and you get incredible information. (personal communication)

Joanne's comment addresses the usefulness of PD-1 and defines its function as a learning space, as Cathy had previously indicated. Joanne pointed out that she learned from PD-1 not only by reading the messages, but also by engaging in the conversations with other attorneys. She substituted physical interaction with other attorneys to computer-based interactions and stated that the listserv was the "computer equivalent of leaning on each other's doorway." Interestingly, the attorneys in this office do not use e-mail with their immediate co-workers for the same purpose. I asked Joanne about the different uses of e-mail and PD-1:

On e-mail, unless you send it [through] GroupWise, you just send it to one person… most of the time, the messages are directed toward a specific person or a small group. So, I don't think it's quite the same. In the PD-1, it goes to everybody in it. It's like somebody pops up and says something… It's different from you… initiating the conversation. You are overhearing it, and then you can join in. (personal communication)

The public defenders in this office clearly distinguished between the use of e-mail and PD-1. Although they could use the office-wide e-mail for the same purpose as PD-1 (i.e., to discuss legal issues and cases), this was not happening. One explanation for this difference is that some attorneys want to be able to choose whether a discussion is "public" and on the listserv, or private and limited to select e-mail recipients. Joanne explained the reasons for some attorneys' attitudes towards PD-1:

There are some attorneys who think it's like a gripe session at the bar, but it's really more substantial – although attorneys' gripe session at the bar is substantial because you are talking about the work… I don't respond often, just occasionally. And I think everybody sort of does occasionally, but there are so many people involved. Now, I run on lots of hard copy from stuff on PD-1. It's very useful. (personal communication)

This kind of socialization seems necessary for the development of professional identities, which I will discuss later in more detail. According to Joanne, everybody takes turns responding to messages, which, in her mind, eliminated the pressure to respond to every post. Although Joanne said she did not respond often, she was an active participant in the discussions on PD-1. In fact, when I was interviewing her, her computer beeped several times, indicating new e-mail messages. She checked her account repeatedly and sometimes told me that the message was from PD-1.

The discussion on PD-l sometimes extends to face-to-face communication. For example, when I was participating in a criminal bar association meeting at a local bar, an attorney raised a question, and another asked her whether she had checked PD-l. This dialogue indicated that these attorneys knew what had been discussed on PD-l and considered it to be a useful resource. David Stevens, a D felony attorney, mentioned a conversation with a friend, also an attorney, and said, "One of the reasons why I know Peter Bruce uses it [PD-l] is because... we hang out and we talk about it. 'Hey, I saw you down there. That was a good response, blah, blah, blah'" (personal communication). These conversations show that online discussions can foster face-to-face communication. At the same time, as with any kind of electronic discussion group, PD-l has drawbacks. Angela Myers, one of the major felony attorneys, did not think that PD-l was an essential resource:

> I'm sort of leaning toward not [using it]. To me, PD-l has a great potential to be a place where lawyers who don't want to do the work can just get on and say, "Hey, tell me what to say, tell me how to do this." Now that's not always bad, but I tend to think that it may stifle younger lawyers from knowing how to research the statutes and knowing how to dig into case law and knowing it... For complicated issues, yeah it's great. I'll tell you the other thing that it has provided for a lot of attorneys. Not particularly full-time here but private practitioners will use it to say, "Look I've got a case in Pentagon County, it's this judge, I've got this issue, tell me what to expect." So people on the PD-l who have gone to Pentagon County... say, "This is his position," or "This is my experience." That's real helpful. (personal communication)

In the above statement, Angela cautions that PD-l has the potential to ruin opportunities for less experienced attorneys to conduct research by themselves because the listserv is only for question-and-answer sessions, not for research. The danger of relying on the information from PD-l too much without critically judging its quality also exists. Alex Gordon, supervisor of the major felony attorneys in Circle County, warned that attorneys need to be selective about the information that can be obtained through PD-l. Attorneys who use PD-l need to evaluate the quality of the information obtained through it. Both Alex and Angela mentioned that their criterion for judging the information on the listserv was based on the reputation of the message sender (e.g., whether that person was a good courtroom attorney). Unlike younger attorneys who have not been practicing long enough to possess such knowledge, both Alex and Angela have been in the field long enough to know most of the other attorneys by name/username and their reputations.

In summary, attorneys use PD-l for many purposes: to ask questions, share updated information, brainstorm strategies, discuss current legal issues, and learn from the discussions. As will be covered in the rest of this chapter, the characteristics of PD-l resemble the attributes of the communities of practice I identified in Section 4.8, and the listserv appears to support sharing of "book knowledge" in particular. On the other hand, there are some components of communities of practice that do not exist in this online example. For instance, it is difficult to confirm that these defense attorneys develop a shared vision because all members of the community are not necessarily full-time public defenders.

6.2 Online Communities of Practice for Other Professions

Online discussion forums, such as the PD-1 listserv, help to cultivate online communities of practice. However, attorneys, especially less experienced public defenders, do not seem to develop a shared vision or gain cultural knowledge, such as a sense of professional identity, via participation in the listserv. Because creation of online communities of practice is becoming prevalent, it is vital that we understand the nature of these communities, including the types of knowledge are shared within them and what makes them sustainable.

6.2.1 Sites Descriptions

My colleague Khe Hew and I analyzed data drawn primarily from three online communities of practice (advanced nursing practice, university Web development, and literacy education) for a series of studies (Hara & Hew, 2007; Hew & Hara, 2007a; Hew & Hara, 2007b). These three professions were chosen based on two considerations. First, I identified professional fields that were rapidly changing and in which there was a need for continuous learning. As shown in Table 6.1, all three professionals are characterized by the fast pace at which new knowledge emerges. Moreover, I evaluated whether there is a shortage of human resources within a particular profession, because a personnel shortage requires newcomers to be brought up to speed much faster than in fields that do not suffer from a scarcity of human resources. The degree of needs indicated in Table 6.1 is, of course, subjective, not empirical.[1] Since participation in communities of practice is an informal form of learning, I have noted the type of formal education each domain requires and whether formal continuing education is obligatory. Finally, the accessibility of these online communities of practice determined the selection of the research sites.

Table 6.1 Study domains

	IT professionals	Teachers	Health professionals
Pace at which new knowledge emerges	Fast	Fast	Fast
Need for more human resources	High	High	High
Requirement for continuing education	Not required, but ideal	Required	Required
Formal education required	Computer Science or Management of Information Systems degree	Teaching certificate	Nursing degree

[1] See Freeman and Aspray (1999) for a discussion regarding the shortage of IT workers, Angus et al. (2000) with regard to nurses, and Ingersoll and Smith (2003) for teachers.

These three online communities of practice were all facilitated through listservs. The Advanced Practice Nurses listserv (herein called APN-l) is open to all clinical nurse specialists, advanced practice nurses, educators, administrators, physicians, and other professionals interested in advanced practice nursing critical care. APN-l was founded in 1993; at the time of the study, there were more than 1,310 members from all parts of the country participating in various discussions. Another listserv analyzed (herein called WD-l) was for the Web developers responsible for designing, implementing, and maintaining a Web site for a higher education institution. WD-1 was originally founded in the fall of 1997. The personal signatures at the end of posted messages reveal that members of WD-l, like members of APN-1, are geographically dispersed. At the time of the study, there were 2,196 people on WD-l. The Literacy Education listserv (herein called LE-l) serves educators who are interested in issues of literacy, primarily in K-6. LE-1 was originally founded in 1997, and at the time of the study, there were 1,242 geographically dispersed educators subscribing to it.

The three listservs selected satisfy Wenger's (1998) four criteria for communities of practice – practice, community, meaning, and identity. Thus they may be considered online communities of practice, wherein online participation not only serves as an avenue for knowledge sharing situated in the actual context of everyday work experience, but also as an experience which helps reinforce the identity of practicing these professions. The first component of a community of practice is shared *practice* (Wenger, 1998), where members engage in developing a shared repertoire of resources, such as experiences, stories, and tools to solve common problems. The second component of a community of practice is that members engage in discussions and share knowledge, which helps members develop a sense of being a part of a *community*. The third component of a community of practice is *meaningful* learning developed through experience. The fourth component of a community of practice addresses the sense of members' *identity*.

It should be noted that Wenger reduced the above four components into three in a later publication (Wenger, 2001), focusing on the application of information technologies in supporting communities of practice. He kept the first two, practice and community, but combined meaning and identity into domain. Domain refers to a specific area of interest that is shared by the members of a community. While we can only speculate why he changed the characteristics to describe communities of practice, it is possible that Wenger realized the limitation placed on information technologies is strained by support for the development of a sense of identity through online communities of practice.

6.3 Types of Knowledge

Researchers have distinguished between tacit and explicit knowledge (e.g., Nonaka & Toyama, 2005). As discussed in Chapter 4, tacit knowledge is embedded in one's practice and is oftentimes difficult to verbalize, whereas explicit knowledge refers to knowledge that is represented in words, formulas, and procedures. In the context of that discussion, I made a distinction between two broad types of knowledge: book knowledge and practical knowledge.

Book knowledge refers to an individual's awareness of knowledge about facts like statutes, policies, and standards. Practical knowledge refers to book knowledge that is applied in real-world situations, and includes know-how. For example, book knowledge can refer to an understanding of how to use certain statutes or similar prior cases for a specific case in a trial. In addition to these two types of knowledge, another type of knowledge that was alluded to in Chapter 5 was cultural knowledge. The concept of cultural knowledge refers to an understanding both of one's beliefs about a practice and one's professional responsibilities within a practice. For example, when considering the profession of public defenders, cultural knowledge entails beliefs regarding the practice (e.g., I believe that everyone in the U.S. has the constitutional right to legal representation), and professional responsibilities associated with defending accused criminals (e.g., negotiating with prosecutors and judges and developing strategies for trials).

This conceptualization of knowledge types is utilized below to analyze the types of knowledge shared in three online communities of practice. The tacit-explicit knowledge dichotomy mentioned earlier was less suitable because it fails to yield a proper understanding of what constitutes knowledge per se, but instead, merely illustrates that knowledge can be either expressed or remain undeclared (Biggam, 2001).

6.4 Types of Knowledge Shared in Online Communities of Practice

The data for this portion of the study were collected from online messages posted to the three online communities of practice during the first 2 weeks of each month for 3 years. First, the messages were analyzed based on message type. Five common activities were identified within the three online environments: (a) requests, (b) statements of appreciation, (c) announcements, (d) clarification, and (e) knowledge sharing.[2] Among the messages categorized as knowledge sharing, analysis of the thematic units revealed that two types of knowledge were shared in APN-l, WD-l, and LE-l: book knowledge and practical knowledge.[3] Representative excerpts from the raw data are presented below, both to contextualize the empirical results and to show that each sample is supported by data from the participants.

The inclination of listserv participants to share practical knowledge is evidence of the fact that the professionals using APN-l, WD-l, and LE-l are willing to engage in problem solving tasks online. This suggests that the three listservs are flourishing

---

[2] See the detailed explanation of these categories in Appendix B.

[3] In order to determine the consistency of our knowledge type analysis, we had an independent coder randomly code approximately 10% of the data. The agreement of the knowledge type coding was 91%, 93%, and 90% for APN-l, WD-l, and LE-l, respectively.

communities of practice because like the members of successful communities of practice, listserv participants tend to engage in problem solving (Ardichvili et al., 2003).

Practical knowledge, which refers to knowledge related to actual practice, can be classified into one of the following three categories: personal opinion, personal suggestion, and institutional practice:

- Personal Opinion – individual opinion about a problem or issue, not necessarily representing best practices. For example, "I believe that we should always assess the discomfort patients' experience in various encounters."
- Personal suggestion – personally recommended solutions to a problem or issue. For example: "When I teach, I always try to incorporate a human interest element into my lecture because students tend to become more involved."
- Institutional practice – knowledge related to what an institution currently practices or has practiced in the past regarding a problem or issue. For example, "Our school system uses the idea of power outlines to teach note-taking. Finding the main idea and supporting details is the reason behind this approach. We do this in middle school."

A comparison of the types of knowledge shared revealed that the most common was "Institutional Practice" (57.3%) for APN-l, "Personal Opinion" (38.3%) for WD-l, and "Personal Opinion" (44.7%) for LE-l (see Fig. 6.1).

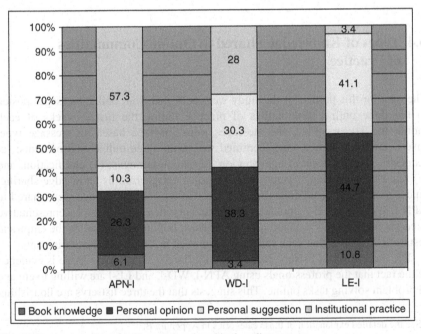

Fig. 6.1 Percentage of types of knowledge shared in three listservs

The relatively low amount of "book knowledge" being shared among the nurses on APN-1 was not very surprising given the fact that many of the members were already very knowledgeable in their respective areas (i.e., a majority of the nurses have advanced degrees in nursing). Typical types of book knowledge shared were the latest policies, regulations, or evidence-based literature pertaining to nursing practice.

The prominence of sharing knowledge relevant to institutional practice by members of APN-1 might be due to current trends in the nursing field that requires advanced practice and critical nurses to base their practice on best practices and research evidence – what Sackett, Straus, Richardson, Rosenberg, and Haynes (2000) refer to as "evidence-based medicine." Evidence-based medicine is the "practice of supporting clinical decision making [via] systematic research, while taking into account the personal values, unique biology, and individual concerns of each patient" (Hendler, 2004, p. 1). The nursing profession is basically a people-oriented profession wherein nurses have direct responsibility for their patients. As such, institutional practice, which refers to knowledge related to an institution's current and/or past practices, might constitute a larger portion of evidence-based medical knowledge than the nurses' own personal opinions and personal suggestions, since it can be assumed that what is actually practiced by a hospital typically will be grounded in current best practices and research evidence. In general, I assume that members in APN-1 would feel more comfortable sharing knowledge relevant to institutional practice because it is something that has already been established by individual institutions.

Unlike APN-1, Web developers on WD-1 shared "Personal Opinion" (38.3%), "Personal Suggestion (30.3%), and "Institutional Practice (28.0%) almost equally. It is possible that knowledge relevant to institutional practice has not become as established among web professionals as has occurred among nursing is because Web development is a relatively new field. It may also stem from the fact that the professionals are engaged in work that changes and evolves much more frequently than nursing. As a consequent of either, both, and/or another reason, many Web developers rely on personal opinions and suggestions from others.

On LE-1, results showed that practical knowledge, namely personal opinions and personal suggestions, was most frequently shared. Because teachers are often isolated (Little, 2002), they may not be as familiar with established institutional practice and thus draw more on their own experience and knowledge. While relatively low counts of book knowledge were shared among the teachers, these individuals shared much more (10.8%) than APN-1 or WD-1 participants. I would speculate that teachers need to follow the changes in legislation pertaining to a professional issue or problem, such as the *No Child Left Behind Act*, and thus book knowledge is shared more than in the other two professions.

It is worth noting that cultural knowledge was not detected in the online messages in any of the above online communities of practice, or in studies of other communities of practice (i.e., digital reference librarians and educational technologists) (Hara, Shachaf, & Stoerger, in preparation). One possible explanation is that cultural knowledge is self-evident: Each member of the communities of practice is involved in a specific profession and voluntarily participates in the online community of practice, which eliminates the need for explicit expressions of such knowledge on the listserv. However, this explanation assumes that each member of online communities of practice has already established a professional identity via cultural knowledge. We cannot always assume that to be the case, as was illustrated in Chapter 5.

It is crucial to acknowledge that the most important component of a community of practice is lacking from online communities of practice (i.e., sharing of cultural knowledge). This is not a major problem for experienced professionals because they have other means for exchanging cultural knowledge and have already internalized cultural knowledge as they gained real-world experience. However, this could be a serious problem for young workers who are new to a profession and have not yet had a chance to obtain much cultural knowledge, much less a sense of professional identity. It is useful for people who undertake projects creating online communities of practice to be aware of this limitation.

6.5 What Makes Knowledge Sharing Sustainable in Online Communities of Practice?

If careful consideration is given to the above limitations, online communities of practice can still be useful for professional development in almost any profession. However, another question that must be asked is what makes online communities of practice sustainable. To investigate the factors that make knowledge sharing sustainable, Khe Hew and I collected interview data from the APN-1 participants (27 nurses – 1 male and 26 female). In this study (Hara & Hew, 2007), the following six factors were identified as being crucial to sustaining knowledge sharing: (1) self-selection, (2) validation of one's practice with others who share a similar working situation, (3) the need to gain a better understanding of current knowledge and best practices in the field, (4) a non-competitive environment, (5) the asynchronous nature of the online communication medium, and (6) the role of the listserv moderator.

Self-selection

Membership self-selection helps reinforce a sense of culture and identity among the members. Furthermore, because self-selection means that members choose to contribute to the community entirely of their own accord, members feel no pressure to share knowledge. As remarked by Bobby, an experienced nurse, in an interview, "Contributing to the APN-1 community is a voluntary thing. People contribute because they want to." Knowledge sharing in the online community of practice thus proceeds informally and naturally.

Validation of one's practice with others who share a similar working situation

A community of practice's domain is defined through its practice. This validation of practice is an important process. Because many members of the APN-l find themselves to be the sole critical care or advanced practice nurse in their organization or town, sharing knowledge in an online community of practice is the only way to connect with like nurses across the country. As Georgia, another experienced nurse, stated, "[Sharing knowledge] helps me to benchmark a lot of practices that I use in my organization."

A need to gain a better understanding of current knowledge and best practices in the field

In addition to providing professional assurance, a community of practice also allows its members to engage in knowledge building. The interview data revealed that the need to be cognizant of the current technology and best practices of their discipline is one of the major challenges many nurses faced in the course of their work. Nurses felt that they gained knowledge as they shared their own. For example, Danielle, a nurse, remarked:

> I think that sharing knowledge is a two-way street. As I share my knowledge, I usually receive some comments and feedback to what I've shared. This back and forth sharing helps me have a better perspective of things. As a result, I gained a better understanding of an issue at the end. (personal communication)

Lesser and Storck's study (2001), which used the local perspective approach, produced findings akin to the current study: participants were able to "respond... more rapidly to customer needs and inquiries" (p. 837). This was analogous to gaining an understanding of current knowledge and best practices.

A non-competitive environment

The very nature of the communication medium also plays an important role in supporting and sustaining an online community of practice. When interviewed, many nurses stated that the online environment helped foster a willingness to share knowledge. This was mainly due to the non-competitive environment afforded by the online communication medium. Traditionally, organizations have rewarded their employees based on individual performance and know-how (Alavi & Leidner, 2001). In such situations, it is expected that individuals will attempt to build up and defend their own accumulated job-related knowledge rather than share it with others (Von Krogh, 1998). However, long-distance, informal contact between professionals from different organizations may provide an important mechanism for overcoming such a barrier (Robertson, Swan, & Newell, 1996; Wasko & Faraj, 2005). The interview data supported this view: some nurses felt that they were able to share knowledge more easily due to the non-competitive character of the distributed online environment simply because they were not all in the same organization. Because there was no competition among them in terms of promotion or reward, nurses felt that they did not have to hoard knowledge. As Jennet, an experienced nurse, remarked:

> I actually get better communication from my peers on the listserv. People are more willing to share things, especially when they are not your peers who may have ulterior motives…trying to work their way up the organization. You know…they [people on the listserv] are not likely to run into you, and so they [are more likely] to tell you an honest opinion. (personal communication)

Asynchronous nature of the online communication medium

The asynchronous medium allows members to communicate with one another at any time and any place. For example, as Amber, a nurse, explained:

> The Internet itself has made it so much easier to let people like us [on the East Coast] to talk to people on the West Coast. You can just like throw something off at the listserv and get people from all over the country to respond to you quickly. It's convenient for the people to respond when they like…it's also convenient for you to pose your question, since you can do it at any time of the day or night you want. (personal communication)

The interview data support the observations made by other researchers, i.e., that listservs have the potential to enhance communication because they are independent of the constraints of place and time that limit traditional face-to-face settings (Althaus, 1997; Harasim, 1987; Quinn, Mehan, Levin, & Black, 1983).

Although the asynchronous nature of using a listserv may help sustain knowledge sharing, it is also important to note that there can be disadvantages associated with its use. The use of a text-based medium can make it difficult for individuals to express certain ideas clearly. For example, Barbara, a nurse with 13 years of experience, explained, "Sometimes I find it difficult to communicate some things clearly in words and I may run the risk of being misunderstood by someone else." Additionally, since knowledge is such an important component of individual self-efficacy and personal self-image, any listserv attacks on an individual's ideas may be viewed as attacks on the individual and damage knowledge sharing (Wasko & Faraj, 2000).

Role of the listserv moderator

Data from the interviews and online observations also indicate that the majority of members perceive the role of the moderator to be pivotal. This finding confirms Gray's (2004) conclusions that the role of a moderator is central to facilitating and sustaining knowledge sharing in an online community. First, APN-1 members appeared to value the moderator's efforts in getting them "up and running" easily and quickly with the new online communication environment when the listserv was migrated. The moderator was observed sending out messages offering personal help to members attempting to access to the new site. It is likely that such forms of assistance helped pave the way for members in APN-1 to be able to use the listserv technology easily. Perceived ease of use is defined as "the degree to which an individual believes that using a particular system would be free of physical and mental effort" (Davis, 1993, p. 477). Perceived usefulness and perceived ease of use of knowledge management system have been identified to have a positive relationship with system use, and as a result, knowledge sharing (Money & Turner, 2004).

By acting as a filter through which all messages are screened before they are posted on the listserv, the moderator also helps keep communication focused on professional issues pertinent to critical care and advanced practice nursing fields. Tiana, an experienced nurse, made the following comment: "[The moderator] is very careful in taking care of the APN-1 discussion." Jannet added, "Personal issues unrelated to the listserv are kept out mainly by the effort of the moderator." An interview with the moderator revealed that commonly rejected messages are those that seek to exploit APN-1 members (e.g., recruitment for self-serving purposes); this does not include genuine job postings, which can be useful for the APN-1 members.

Furthermore, the moderator helps keep communication civil and respectful by acting as a "watchdog" of netiquette. For example, the moderator explained in an interview that unprofessional statements (e.g., personal attacks on a member) are frowned upon, and that she is quick to caution those responsible. The moderator confirmed that such incidents are rare and only seem to occur about once a year.

Table 6.2 presents a comparison of the six factors identified in this research and Wenger's original four characteristics of a community of practice. The first factor, self-selection, resonates with the concept of identity in Wenger's framework. Self-selection is based on an existing identity and is also a precondition to participation in the online community of practice, though this is not something conveyed within the online community of practice itself. The second factor, validation of one's practice, fits neatly within the category of practice in Wenger's framework. The third factor, better understanding of current knowledge and best practice in the field, is embedded in practice, which makes learning meaningful. The fourth and sixth factors,

Table 6.2 Comparison of six factors that sustain knowledge sharing among nurses and Wenger's four characteristics of a community of practice

Factors that sustain knowledge sharing	Wenger's four characteristics of a community of practice
Self-selection	Identity
Validation of one's practice	Practice
Better understanding of current knowledge & best practice in the field	Practice/Meaning
Non-competitive environment	Community
Asynchronous nature of the online communication medium	–
Role of the listserv moderator	Community

a non-competitive environment and the role of the listserv moderator, also help to develop a sense of community. However, the fifth factor, the asynchronous nature of the online communication medium, refers to a characteristic of the technology which does not directly relate to any of Wenger's characteristics. This raises the argument of whether we need to consider the technological characteristics of online communities of practice in addition to the characteristics that Wenger (1998) and his successors developed based on face-to-face communities of practice.

Furthermore, these six factors are quite different from the factors identified by Wasko and Faraj (2005), although two of these factors can be considered closely related to Wasko and Faraj's model. The non-competitive environment (i.e., the fourth factor) may be related to relational capital as identified in Wasko and Faraj's model, although this factor was not explicitly mentioned and supported by the data in their study. Additionally, the sixth factor, regarding the role of the moderator, is applicable to the centrality of structural capital as described in Wasko and Faraj's model. The four other factors (i.e., self-selection, validation of one's practice, a need to gain a better understanding of current knowledge, and asynchronicity of the technology) were not described in Wasko and Faraj's model, thus indicating a possible difference between the *a priori* framework (i.e., Wasko and Faraj's model) and local perspectives (i.e., the findings described here).

6.5.1 Relationships Among the Six Factors

Figure 6.2 identifies possible relationships among the six factors, and groups the factors into constructs. Self-selection and non-competitiveness are inferred to be critical components of the listserv social environment. Validation of practice and the need to gain a better understanding of current knowledge constitute key elements of an individual's needs, and asynchronicity is a key component of the listserv's technological features. Together, these three constructs (i.e., listserv social environment, individual needs, and technological features) sustain knowledge sharing in APN-1.

Self-selection and non-competitiveness may be related to each other by more than the fact that both are part of the social environment. Self-selective membership implies that individuals join a community of practice voluntarily and share knowledge of their own accord. I would speculate that an individual's needs directly influence self-selective membership (see Fig. 6.2). For example, people join APN-1 voluntarily because they need to validate their own professional practice and stay informed of the current technology and best practices in the nursing discipline. It is likely that self-selective membership helps guarantee a more serious group, one which has a genuine interest in the discussion that is taking place (Smith, 2003), and hence is less concerned about the issue of competing for reward or recognition for knowledge contribution. Furthermore, the listserv moderator can be considered a watchdog of self-selective membership, helping to ensure that inappropriate individuals (e.g., advertisers and spammers) are kept out.

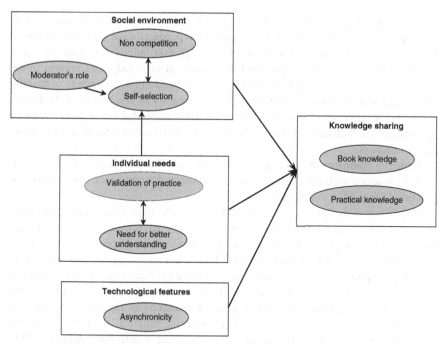

Fig. 6.2 Possible relationships among the six identified factors

Validation of one's own practice and the need to gain a better understanding of the current knowledge and best practices in the field may also influence each other. It is likely that cognizance of current best practices can help one better benchmark one's own practice with that of other nurses in the field.

6.6 Commentary

This chapter has focused on online communities of practice. One of these communities of practice formed within the context of the listserv for public defenders in Shape State. Although all of the office attorneys did not participate in this listserv, those who had joined it found it very useful. The attorneys used the listserv for at least two different purposes. The first use was to brainstorm cases with other attorneys who are not necessarily located in the same office. Some major felony attorneys who participated in the listserv indicated that it provided a sense of a community for public defenders. The second use was to learn about updated information from discussions on the listserv. This second usage appeared to have been especially helpful for less experienced attorneys, although experienced attorneys cautioned that one must carefully consider the integrity of the information posted on the listserv. Additionally, some attorneys indicated that the listserv seemed very useful for public defenders in rural areas because they do not typically have access to experienced criminal attorneys.

The study of online communities of practice in three professions (nurses, web developers, and literacy educators) expanded the perspective of knowledge sharing by categorizing the different types of knowledge that individuals share with one another. The analysis shows that book and practical knowledge are present in the online discussions, but cultural knowledge is not. In addition, six factors of making knowledge sharing sustainable in an online community of practice from the participants' perspective were identified. These findings are useful not only to advanced practice nurses, Web developers, and literacy educators, but also to other professions and researchers.

Table 6.3 compares the original four components Wenger identified for communities of practice with the characteristics of online and face-to-face communities of practice addressed in this book.

Online communities of practice do not possess the same characteristics as face-to-face communities of practice. In particular, the presence of two of the characteristics, development of shared meaning and development of professional identity, are questionable in online environments. This is evidenced by the lack of cultural knowledge sharing. Of course, online communities of practice can supplement face-to-face interaction. Agre (1998) suggests that "a community has to meet in person, eat and drink as a group, discuss various formulations of the shared vision that brings them together, engage in concrete collective projects," and that electronic media may have a role to in supporting some of these activities. Although PD-l served to create a sense of community among defense attorneys in Shape State, there are some activities that computer-mediated communication does not support well, such as socialization in task-specific online environments and in the transmission of tacit knowledge. Cooney's (1998) study of 10th-grade English students using Internet Relay Chat (IRC) found that the students tended not to engage in "off-task talk." Off-task talk plays a crucial socialization role in online discussions in order to create a shared meaning. Thus, when people are assigned to a specific task (e.g.,

Table 6.3 Comparison of characteristics for communities of practice

Face-to-face Community of Practice identified in this book	Online Community of Practice identified in this book	Wenger (1998)
A group of professional practitioners	A group of professional practitioners	Practice
Informal networks	Informal networks	Community
Supportive culture	Supportive culture	Community
Engagement in knowledge building	Engagement in knowledge building only for book and practical knowledge, not cultural knowledge	Practice
Development of shared meaning		Meaning
Development of professional identities	Reinforcement (not development) of professional identity	Identity

discussion of criminal cases or class discussion) and to a certain virtual environment (e.g., PD-1 or IRC), they may not be inclined to use the environment for other purposes (e.g., socialization or transmission of tacit knowledge).

Online communities of practice among attorneys, as well as other professionals, function in a similar manner to face-to-face communities of practice; however, online communities of practice seem to supplement elements of the face-to-face communities of practice rather than providing an equally robust alternative to such communities. In the next chapter, I will expand on the characteristics of communities of practice in order to expand our understanding of the concept. I will also consider the relationship between communities of practice and IT, and the implications of these studies for further research and development.

Chapter 7
Toward an Understanding of Communities of Practice

This chapter will present cross-case analyses and link findings from the study to the literature on organizational learning, communities of practice, and information science. First, the characteristics of communities of practice will be described with regard to the two major functions of CoPs: social construction of knowledge and the creation of opportunities for the development of professional socialization and identity. Then, communities of practice and IT integration will be presented in order to discuss the role of IT in the different types of communities of practice examined in Chapters 4–6 (i.e., a community of practice in Square County, two communities of practice in Circle County, and online communities of practice). Following the discussion of the ways in which IT can support communities of practice, implications of these studies for further research and development in the following three areas will be discussed: education, information science, and communities of practice.

7.1 Characteristics of Communities of Practice

7.1.1 Social Construction of Knowledge in Communities of Practice: Three Kinds of Knowledge

In a community of practice, various types of knowledge can be shared. Three types of knowledge are articulated here: cultural knowledge and two kinds of subject-matter knowledge – practical and book knowledge (see the knowledge typology in Table 7.1). In some communities of practice, the subject matter changes rapidly (e.g., communities of practice for lawyers or IT professionals). Consider the fact that among database administrators normalization of database structure was a requirement for many years; advances in processors and the present availability of cheap hardware, however, led some to assert that normalization was not as important as it was in the past (cf., Kottke, 2004). Such alterations in a profession's foundational understanding demonstrate the importance of the rapidly changing nature of knowledge in communities of practice. Moreover, organizational culture can change

Table 7.1 Knowledge typology in communities of practice

Professional identity	Cultural knowledge	Tacit
	Practical knowledge	
Subject-matter knowledge		Explicit
	Book knowledge	

rapidly, perhaps because of a high turnover rate. The original definition of a community of practice proposed by Lave and Wenger (1991) appeared to refer only to static cultural knowledge and subject-matter knowledge because those studies examined communities that had existed for a significant period of time. However, many jobs now require workers to master subject matter that is evolving rapidly. Therefore, it is imperative that we address the learning of rapidly changing subject-matter knowledge in communities of practice.

In this book, cultural knowledge refers to what it is like to be a member of a certain profession (e.g., a public defender). As such, we have focused on the development of professional identity (see Chapter 5). The tacit knowledge necessary for an individual to become a full member of a community of practice is embedded in the culture of the workplace. For example, younger attorneys learn how to be public defenders by observing more experienced attorneys and by talking with them. As Huseman and Goodman (1999) state, "culture is one of the most powerful stores of knowledge" (p. 121).

We have classified subject-matter knowledge as either book knowledge or practical knowledge (see the knowledge typology in Table 7.1). Book knowledge refers to factual knowledge, such as empirical information gained via encyclopedic awareness of historical case laws and statutes.[1] In contrast, practical knowledge refers to real-world application of book knowledge; for example, knowing how to use precedents identified in LexisNexis or Westlaw in a bench trial. Attorneys learn most of their book knowledge in law school, but they also are required to continue acquiring new book knowledge because criminal laws are rapidly changing. In addition, the attorneys have to learn how to use their book knowledge, a process that leads to the conversion of book knowledge into practical knowledge.

To understand how book knowledge is assimilated as practical knowledge, which is easily shared with other people, I would propose the application of Actor-Network Theory (e.g., Callon, 1995; Latour, 1987). Actor-Network Theory describes relationships within social networks. Latour developed this theory to explain how scientific knowledge is shared and constructed among scientists working in labs. The most intriguing aspect of this theory is the inclusion of artifacts into social networks as a means for the construction of shared knowledge. According to Actor-Network Theory, artifacts influence the construction of knowledge to the same degree that people do, an observation that led Latour and his colleagues to coin the term

---

[1] Of course, when considering statutes and case law, there is room for interpretation. However, in order to arrive at reasoned interpretations, one needs this book knowledge.

"actants." For example, in Section 4.3: Collective Knowledge Building, I described that the precedent that Richard found helped other attorneys in his office with cases involving the BMV. In this situation, the case (an actant) played a major role in assisting the public defenders' work. How such a case is used among the attorneys plays an important role in constructing shared knowledge, as does the human network existing among the attorneys. In the Public Defender's Office in Circle County, actants are more complex because the office contains more people using a wider range of artifacts and tools (e.g., Patio, Internet, and PD-1), to support their work practices. For example, attorneys share their experience and knowledge via PD-1. These electronic mediums functions as a learning aid in addition to providing a forum that enables participants to construct their own knowledge about legal practice by interacting with other attorneys.

Reiffenstein (2006) contends that the communities of practice literature primarily focuses on tacit knowledge but includes only a limited discussion on "codified" [explicit] knowledge. He suggests that using Actor-Network Theory will help us better understand the conversion of tacit and "codified" knowledge. For example, when filing a patent, inventors most make their tacit knowledge accessible as explicit knowledge. In addition, Fox (2000) argues that the issue of power is rarely addressed in the community of practice literature and has proposed the use of Actor-Network Theory to articulate power issues. Other studies have synthesized the frameworks of communities of practice and Actor-Network Theory, and this may be a fruitful means to deepen our understanding of tacit and explicit knowledge.

The group that I studied in Square County happened to be one that already had a well-established community; the youngest attorney had been in the office for about 6 years. Thus, the concept of a community of practice as originally defined was potentially problematic for this study, primarily because Lave and Wenger's (1991) concept of a community of practice focused on newcomers learning the knowledge embedded in a community but did not focus on established members of a community of practice. Hence, the gist of the original concept was on the process of becoming a full member of the community. Still, although the group I studied did not have a newcomer, a robust community of practice did exist among these public defenders. Since culture in an existing community is not static (Van Mannen, 1988), not only newcomers but also full members of a community must continue to learn the culture, in addition to learning *in* the culture.

For example, I had a chance to participate in a management retreat of the Circle County's Public Defender's Office. The managers discussed how the culture of the office had changed as the number of employees had increased. They started with 10 full-time attorneys and 2 secretaries in 1994. At that time, all of them were very close. Several years later, the office had grown to approximately 50 full-time attorneys, 60 contract attorneys, and 50 support staff employees. Because of this, the employees no longer knew each other as well. The managers also discussed the problems I identified in Chapter 5 relevant to the physical separation of the less experienced and seasoned attorneys and proposed restructuring task divisions to overcome problems inherent in this organization. This attempt to restructure would likely change the culture of the office yet again, hopefully in such a way as to mix experienced and less experienced attorneys into shared communities of practice. This would further the sharing and construction of all three kinds of knowledge supported by communities of practice: book knowledge, practical knowledge, and cultural knowledge.

7.1.2 Why it Does Not Support Identity Formation

Cultural knowledge and aspects of practical knowledge are tacit. As a result, the primary mechanism of learning relies on observing experts. Lave has proposed that culture is "the reproduction of ways of being in the world" (cited in Rival, 1996, p. 164). Along the same lines, Rival illustrates two communities of practice in a village school and a rural longhouse, and states that "culture is not primarily acquired through the internalization of norms and values, or the transmission of factual information and abstract skills, but through interactive learning" (p. 164). The best way to learn tacit practical knowledge is to observe others, especially more experienced co-workers, and to apply that knowledge in practice. Interaction with other workers (socialization) plays a major role in the learning of cultural knowledge. By means of everyday practices and interactions with colleagues, employees share, construct, and obtain cultural knowledge.

On the other hand, some aspects of practical knowledge and book knowledge are explicit (i.e., they can be shared through documents and in electronic formats, such as messages on a listserv). Studies presented in Chapter 6 found that listservs or online discussions provide some subject-matter knowledge that is explicit, but fail to provide much cultural knowledge and tacit practical knowledge. While some listservs do create a sense of a community among professionals, CMC generally does not support activities like socialization in task-specified online environments and the transmission of tacit knowledge. Off-task talk facilitates socialization in online discussions in order to create shared meaning. As discussed earlier, online discussions rarely possess off-task types of behavior (Cooney, 1998).

In terms of the transmission of tacit knowledge, Roberts (2000) and Brown and Duguid (1993) argue that tacit knowledge is difficult to transfer through electronic media because such media tend to lack rich interpersonal communication. Therefore, tacit knowledge may not be useful in explicit forms.[2]

7.1.3 Professional Socialization and Identity

One of the roles that communities of practice play is to provide an environment for professional socialization within which members may develop professional identity.

---

[2] Nonaka's (1994) conversion model also includes human effort to transfer tacit knowledge to explicit knowledge. In his model, explicit knowledge can be distributed via technologies once the knowledge goes through an "externalization" process (i.e., conversion of tacit knowledge).

Having colleagues with whom to exchange ideas is an important factor leading to participation in a community of practice (Singer, 1982; Weedman, 1999). Su (1992), who has written about the importance of mentoring and socialization for preservice teachers, has also reported that preservice teachers find informal interactions, such as meeting with professors for meals, retreats, weekend gatherings, to be vital because they gain more useful information via informal talks and discussions than they do from formal seminars. His findings are consistent with earlier studies (e.g., Parsons, 1939), as well as with Brown and Duguid's (1991) assertion regarding the importance of informal learning (see Chapter 2 for details). As Lave (1988) says, "Everyday practice is a more powerful source of socialization than intentional pedagogy" (p. 14).

Singer (1982) has argued about the significance of developing one's self within the professional community. He has also noted that although book knowledge is provided, most training programs do not assist students with understanding the roles of professionals in the real world; rather, participants require opportunities for informal socialization in order to learn the professional identity of a particular profession. As Su (1992) puts it, "Socialization is a mutually influential process" (p. 247) for many professionals, including public defenders, high-energy physicists (Traweek, 1988), librarians (Davenport, 2001), and teachers (Su, 1992).

In two of the Public Defender's Offices, I examined the way the attorneys learned about their profession by socializing with other attorneys. However, my observations found that socialization occurred only among those attorneys who were physically located in the same place. To help extend a sense of community among public defenders, computer conferencing tools, such as listservs, can be used to offer opportunities for socialization. Still, although the existing listserv, PD-l, provides a forum for knowledge sharing, it does not appear to be useful for helping to develop the professional identity of a public defender. This finding was supported by studies of other listservs used by professionals to share knowledge, as described in Chapter 6. There was no evidence to support the supposition that professionals were sharing cultural knowledge in the listservs. As mentioned previously, the overly task-specific nature of listservs may hinder the ability of the medium to support socialization.

7.1.4 Organizational Learning and Communities of Practice

As described in Chapter 2, discussions of organizational learning in the professional literature contain two perspectives: the cognitive perspective and the cultural perspective. Although Brown and Duguid (1991) imply that a relationship between organizational learning and communities of practice exists, they do not explicitly specify this perspective in their article. I, on the other hand, have come to realize that a community of practice is an environment in which organizational learning based mostly on the cultural perspective occurs.

Moreover, Lave and Wenger (1991) originally defined communities of practice as scaffolding that allows newcomers to a workplace or other settings to become part of the community or profession. Newcomers begin as peripheral members and eventually become full-fledged members of the community. This interpretation makes sense if one considers communities of practice from an anthropological perspective (i.e. within a framework of enculturation). For example, consider how an infant may grow to become a full member of a community/tribe. If true (and I believe it is), then it would appear that Lave and Wenger's emphasis is on the development of "cultural knowledge," including identity, which is embedded in the community.

In Chapter 1 Section 1.1.2, I defined communities of practice as "collaborative, informal networks that support professional practitioners in their efforts to develop shared understandings and engage in work-relevant knowledge building." Based on this definition, five attributes of communities of practice were elaborated upon in Chapter 2: (1) a CoP is composed of a group of professional practitioners; (2) a CoP helps foster the development of a shared meaning; (3) CoPs are made up of informal networks; (4) CoPs provide a supportive culture; and (5) members of a CoP engage in knowledge building. I would note here a sixth attribute of communities of practice: (6) they lead to the development of professional identities.

A community of practice provides an informal learning environment in which both novices and experienced members of a professional community may interact with each other, share their experiences, and learn from each other. In this sense, organizational learning occurs in a community of practice. Furthermore, it is plain that novices learn how to be professionals by being mentored and apprenticed to more experienced members. This perspective encapsulates the concept of "legitimate peripheral participation" as developed by Lave and Wenger (1991). In using this term, they argue that "learners inevitably participate in communities of practitioners and that mastery of knowledge and skill requires newcomers to move toward full participation in the sociocultural practices of a community" (p. 29). In the Public Defender's Office in Circle County, new attorneys learned how to practice law by means of legitimate peripheral participation in the misdemeanor/D felony courts and eventually moved up to become major felony attorneys, a shift that led to their full-participation in the community of public defenders.

However, communities of practice are useful not only for novices. Learning is a continuing process in any profession. Although Lave and Wenger (1991) do not address the fact that learning occurs among full members of a community, my observations found that even experienced attorneys who have been practicing for more than 15 years can learn from younger attorneys because a conversation with less experienced attorneys elicits the experienced attorneys' reflections on their own actions. A community of practice provides a setting that bridges these two groups (novice and experienced) and enables them to start a conversation within a particular profession.

One problem with the concept of "legitimate peripheral participation" is that it is hard to draw a line between novices and experienced people (i.e., how do we determine when we have full-participation?). Thom Ashton, one of the public defenders in Square County, mentioned that he never felt that he had peaked as an attorney, though others perceived him as a very experienced attorney. However, his statement makes sense, given that one reason for participation in a community of practice is to learn continuously. Thus, the self-perception of not having "peaked" may be a driving force that keeps more experienced members active in the community. Of course, there are other possible factors that keep them in a community of practice. They may seek emotional solidarity, or perhaps they have a desire to pass on experience to younger generations.

Communities of practice provide milieus for professionals to learn from each other and become better at their profession. A professional practice provides the framework for a community of practice because a community of practice, by definition, emerges around a particular field of practice. I found the development of professional identity to be one of the most important components of face-to-face communities of practice. A groups' sense of professional identity makes or breaks a community of practice.

7.2 Communities of Practice & IT Integration

Harasim (1990) advocates the possibility of extension of "personal/professional networks into a global community" (p. 46) by using computer-mediated communication. Many authors (e.g., Harasim, 1990, 1993; Sharp, 1997; Sproull & Kiesler, 1991) assert that computer networks should be used to build, expand, and support a virtual community. In fact, some authors (e.g., Hara, Bonk, & Angeli, 2000; Haythornthwaite & Kazmer, 2004; Josefsson, 2005; Weedman, 1999) discuss the development of a sense of community among students who communicate online. However, in order to build a virtual community of practice, we need to carefully design the learning environment by considering all the technical, pedagogical, and organizational issues. Brown and Duguid (1995) make the point that it is difficult to form a virtual community of practice, though electronic communication fosters the expansion of existing communities.

Based on the study of communities of practice presented in this book, the relationship between communities of practice and the use of information technologies is not necessarily strong. In other words, use of IT does not necessarily strengthen a community of practice. In fact, the higher the self-proclaimed use of information technologies, the weaker the ties were found to be between the people using them. This finding is somewhat inconsistent with claims made by authors who assert that IT connects people (e.g., Sproull & Kiesler, 1991).

As mentioned earlier, the Public Defender's Office in Square County appeared to have a stronger community of practice than that found in Circle County. One reason for this might be the size of the organization. Barker (1960) proposed the Behavior Setting Theory and compared small and large organizations; he argued that people in small organizations tend to have a stronger sense of satisfaction, participate in a wider range of activities, and have more responsibilities for assigned tasks because they were under-resourced. The Behavior Setting Theory may explain the difference between offices in this study. However, small organizations have some disadvantages as well. Barker notes that "the underpopulated setting is one where self-esteem and social status can both flourish, and also wither" (p. 33). Because undermanned settings do not have enough human resources, individuals' responsibilities become heavier than in a large organization. Consequently, while individuals in a small organization have more opportunities to develop high self-esteem and social status (as in the Public Defender's Office in Square County), because of the lack of human resources, there is also a risk that members will not be able to accomplish tasks effectively (as in the communities of practice that exists among the less experienced attorneys in Circle County).

7.2.1 Differences between Online and Face-to-Face Communities of Practice

Online communities of practice, like those that develop around listservs or online discussion forums, provide explicit subject-matter knowledge but often fail to provide cultural knowledge. As such, online communities of practice accommodate some aspects of face-to-face communities of practice, but not all of them. As described earlier, many aspects of communities of practice can be cultivated online. The online communities of practice described in Chapter 6 tend to support the following attributes: (1) a CoP is composed of a group of professional practitioners; (3) CoPs are made up of informal networks; (4) CoPs provide a supportive culture; and (5) members of a CoP engage in knowledge building. On the other hand, the studies did not reveal whether online communities of practice contain the following attributes: (2) they help foster the development of a shared meaning, and (6) they lead to the development of professional identities. This finding challenges the notion that communities of practice can be supported by online environments (e.g., Wenger, 2001). Despite the fact that some attributes of communities of practice, namely specific types of knowledge sharing, are supported by online communities of practice, there is no evidence that other important attributes – development of shared meaning and professional identities – are present in online communities of practice.

Whittaker and Schwarz (1999) reported on an ethnographic study of the software developers using electronic scheduling software. They concluded that current scheduling software is not appropriate for coordinating software development and indicated its limitations, which involved social and motivational factors. As found in their study, the role of IT can be suitable for certain tasks, but not all tasks. Hence, it is unlikely that online communities of practice will provide a substitute for face-to-face communities of practice.

To my knowledge, there has been no discussion of the disadvantages of developing communities of practice in online environments; the discourse seems to focus only on the advantages found therein. We need to start identifying the limitations of online communities of practice and accommodate to use IT accordingly.

7.3 Implications of this Study for Further Research and Development

7.3.1 Implications for Education

The results of the study presented in this book may be useful in a number of ways. First, researchers who study organizational learning and communities of practice can benefit from this study's local theory. Wenger (1998) developed a broad theoretical framework of communities of practice that consisted of practice and identity. We need to expand his framework and examine more details of individual communities of practice both online and offline. Second, the results of the studies would be of obvious benefit to any professional organization. By understanding the nature of a community of practice and of organizational learning, an organization can make practices more productive and effective. Finally, this study provides a new view on learning that should be of interest to educators and trainers (i.e., teaching professionals), who tend to focus more on formal training than informal learning.

7.3.2 Implications for Information Science

To what degree can information technologies support communities of practice? Some IT can be used to bring people together. A networked IT application can provide an environment for both novice and experienced researchers to interact with and learn from each other, thus providing "legitimate peripheral participation" to novices. Furthermore, researchers at different locations can share their concerns and experiences with colleagues at other locations by using online conferencing tools as seen in the APN-1 example. They can be counselors for each other, and they can collectively solve problems. These exchanges have the potential to be beneficial for novices because the experienced researchers' "tacit knowledge" would be more explicitly available to them. Novices might then be able to gain contextualized practical knowledge in addition to book knowledge. They can learn to become "reflective practitioners" (Schön, 1983) and full members of a community of practice (Lave & Wenger, 1991) by observing the conversations of experienced researchers. In addition, whereas instant messaging tends to be used mainly for informal conversations (cf., Nardi, Whittaker, & Bradner, 2000), it could stimulate spontaneous knowledge sharing. Regardless, as noted earlier, fostering cultural knowledge among the members of such a community would be a challenge in an online environment, and, though technologies have evolved since the data in this study were collected, these issues persist.

Moreover, we cannot overlook the importance of fostering an environment that encourages knowledge sharing. Six factors (self-selection; validation of one's practice; better understanding of current knowledge and practice; non-competitive environment; asynchronous nature of the online medium; role of the moderator) for a sustainable knowledge sharing community identified in Chapter 6 can be used as a guideline to foster new or existing online communities of practice. In addition, Desouza (2003) describes a study of an IT company that provided game rooms where employees were able to socialize. After several weeks of hesitation, employees began to use the game rooms to interact with peers and exchange practical knowledge. Desouza found an increase in project-based knowledge contributions after the installation of the game rooms. Plaskoff (2003) also notes that one of the critical factors in designing a community of practice is to have discussions about what it means to be part of a community, not only a professional community of practice but also churches, neighborhoods, schools, etc., before joining such a community. These discussions can illuminate reasons for participating, and thus, people may be more likely to continue participating in the community. I believe that more attention needs to be paid to the design of environments before designing IT tools to support communities of practice.

In practice, administrators of organizations can use the coding schema described in Chapter 6 to gauge the current activities (e.g., types of activities and knowledge) of existing online communities of practice. Future research should also examine the perceptions and opinions of members who have since left online environments in order to have a more comprehensive understanding of the motivators and barriers of knowledge sharing. Future studies can be expanded to other online environments involving other professional practices to see whether the findings in this study apply.

7.3.3 Implications for Communities of Practice

As Brown and Duguid (1993) indicate, whether one can design or operationalize situated learning is a difficult question because "where 'situated learning' talks of *learning*, questions about educational technology tend to be framed around *teaching* and instruction" (p. 10, original emphasis). How to best design learning environments so that learners develop professionally in social contexts is a question that is continually debated in the education and training professions. Brown and Duguid (1993) have suggested that designers and instructors create a learning environment in which learners are allowed to "steal" appropriate knowledge. In addition to their suggestions, we need to consider what factors help to create autonomous, self-motivated learners because placing learners in the middle of a rich practice does not always encourage them to "steal" the knowledge necessary for their own practice. For example, when the Circle County Public Defender's Office placed experienced and inexperienced attorneys in the same court, it was questionable whether less experienced attorneys were eager to steal (learn) knowledge from more experienced attorneys because a successful learning experience depends on the self-motivation of the less experienced attorneys. In this book, I identified that much of the public defenders' motivation comes from professional pride and willingness to help their clients. Therefore, the question is: how we can facilitate this professional pride and the development of professional identities? While I have offered potential solutions, we need to continue searching for answers to this question.

A community of practice involves both work and learning. Currently, educators are overly excited about communities of practice, and the process of, what they call "creating" a learning community.[3] However, a community of practice and a learning community are different concepts. I argue, in agreement with Wenger (1998), that "learning cannot be designed: it can only be designed for – that is, facilitated or frustrated" (p. 229). Additionally, Wenger indicated that a learning community is helpful for newcomers. I would like to emphasize that this type of community is also useful for experienced workers because experienced workers can learn from novices, share experience with their colleagues, and engage in brainstorming. In communities of practice, learning is implicit. In order to improve their work practices, workers have to learn new things continuously. Learning is, in fact, embedded in the practice.

I believe that future research of communities of practice should be based on Wenger's (1998) theorization of the concept, which is rooted in social theory. This framework is crucial to our understanding of communities of practice. Certainly the concept of communities of practice receives much attention from different fields, including education and information science; yet empirical research on communities of practice is still relatively sparse. This book contributes significantly to the field because it adds another empirical examination.

7.4 Epilogue

In this book, I focused on collective learning within the context of communities of practice. I have attempted to illustrate communities of practice in two Public Defender's Offices as well as three online communities of practice. Each community of practice has its own unique attributes. Yet, I found that there are several common elements that make up all communities of practice: (1) they are made up of a group of practitioners; (2) they foster the development of a shared meaning; (3) they are composed of informal networks; (4) they are a precursor to supportive and trusting culture; (5) their members engage in knowledge building; and (6) they assist individuals in the negotiation and development of professional identities. Furthermore, in order to form a community of practice, members have to learn continuously, and thus, autonomy is another important aspect of a community of practice. In the communities of public defenders, the attorneys I studied in Square County shared a common vision – to help their clients. To accomplish this goal, they tried to improve their own practice through interactions with their colleagues.

Additionally, I examined the use of IT in the Public Defender's Office in Circle County. These attorneys used IT to support three categories of social action: instrumental, communicative, and discursive. The study did not find a strong relationship

---

[3] See Brown and Duguid (1993).

between communities of practice and IT. The listservs APN-l, WD-l, and LE-l, used by different types of professions, help to create online communities of practice, but these listservs did not seem to support the development of cultural knowledge. However, these online communities could potentially be supplemented by face-to-face interactions among local professionals.

This book provides empirical studies that at times led to conclusions that come into conflict with earlier claims about IT and communities of practice. The concept of community of practice is a rich and complex subject, and this book has revealed new perspectives on the concept. I feel that this book lays the foundation for a theory of informal learning, and, more specifically, an understanding of the roles of communities of practice and IT in the sphere of informal learning.

Appendix A: Cast of Characters

Table A.1 People in Square County

Name	Division/Title
Paul Linton	Manager
Thom Ashton	Attorney
Richard Williams	Attorney
Alisha Brown	Attorney
Nick Carter	Attorney
Sally Martin	Attorney
Jason Oliver	Attorney
Vicky Peterson	Secretary
Ben Rogers	Defendant
Matt White	Defendant
Ben Wagner	Defendant
Jim Graham	Defendant

Table A.2 People in Circle County

Name	Division/Title
Michael Taylor	Chief public defender
Nancy Cooper	Training Director
Alex Gordon	Supervisor of major felony division
Gina Dean	Major felony
Elizabeth Fox	Major felony
Joanne Kent	Major felony
Roy Stewart	Major felony
Rhonda Smith	Supervisor of misdemeanor/D felony
Cathy Bruce	Misdemeanor
Linda Ellis	Misdemeanor
Ann Howard	Misdemeanor/D felony
Harry Johnson	D felony
David Stevens	D felony

Table A.3 Nurses on APN-1

Name	Years of experience	Years on APN-1
Tiana	25	8
Jannet	21	1.5
Bobby	25	9 months
Amber	18	4
Barbara	13	1.5
Georgia	27	1
Danielle	8	2

Appendix B: Types of Activities

a. Request – request for help or ideas. For example: "How are you discarding empty bottles that have the patient's information on them?"
b. Appreciation – offering thanks for some action. For example: "Thank you for all the work it took to do this for us."
c. Announcement – spreading word about job openings or conference registrations. For example: "We are seeking at least two full-time nurse practitioners."
d. Clarification – giving more pertinent details about a request for help. For example: "I just need to clarify one thing on my request for information. Although we do use XXX bed occasionally, my question was regarding the YYY bed."
e. Knowledge sharing – sharing book knowledge or practical knowledge.

References

Aeppel, T. (2002, July 1). Tricks of the trade: On factory floors, top workers hide secrets to success. *The Wall Street Journal*, p. A1.

Agre, P. (1998). Networking on the network. Crossroads: The ACM student magazine. Retrieved June 16, 2008 from http://www.acm.org/crossroads/xrds4-4/network.html

Alavi, M., Leidner, D. E. (2001). Knowledge management and knowledge management systems: Conceptual foundations and research issues. *MIS Quarterly, 25*(1), 107–136.

Alter, S. (2006). *Goals and tactics on the dark side of knowledge management.* Paper presented at the Proceedings of the 39th Hawaii International Conference on System Sciences.

Althaus, S. (1997). Computer-mediated communication in the university classroom: An experiment with online discussions. *Communication Education, 46*(3), 158–174.

Angus, D. C., Kelly, M. A., Schmitz, R. J., White, A., Popovich, J. J. (2000). Current and projected workforce requirements for care of the critically ill and patients with pulmonary disease: Can we meet the requirements of an aging population?" *Journal of the American Medical Association, 284*(21), 2762–2770.

Ardichvili, A., Page, V., & Wentling, T. (2003). Motivation and barriers to participation in online knowledge–sharing communities of practice. *Journal of Knowledge Management, 7*(1), 64–77.

Argyris, C. (1991). Teaching smart people how to learn. *Harvard Business Review*, 99–109.

Bandura, A. (1982). Self-efficacy mechanism in human agency. *American Psychologist, 37*(2), 122–147.

Bapuji, H., & Crossan, M. (2004). From questions to answers: Reviewing organizational learning research. *Management Learning, 35*(4), 397–417.

Barker, R. G. (1960). Ecology and motivation. In M. R. Jones (Ed.), *Nebraska symposium on motivation* (pp. 1–49). Lincoln, NE: University of Nebraska Press.

Barth, S. (2000, October). KM horror stories. *Knowledge Management Magazine*, Retrieved April 28, 2006, from http://www.destinationkm.com/articles/default.asp?ArticleID=923

Baskerville, R., & Dulipovici, A. (2006). *The ethics of knowledge transfers and conversations: Property or privacy rights?* Paper presented at the Proceedings of the 39th Hawaii International Conference on System Sciences.

Becker, H. (1960). Becoming a Marihuana mser. In H. Becker (Ed.), *Outsiders: Studies in the sociology of deviance* (pp. 41–58). Glencoe: Free Press.

Biggam, J. (2001). *Defining knowledge: An epistemological foundation for knowledge management.* Paper presented at the Proceedings of the 34th Hawaii International Conference on System Sciences. Computer Society Press. Available at http://csdl2.computer.org/comp/proceedings/hicss/2001/0981/07/09817070.pdf

Blackler, F. (1995). Knowledge, knowledge work and organizations: An overview and interpretation. *Organization Studies, 16*(6), 1021–1046.

Brown, J. S., Collins, A., & Duguid, P. (1989). Situated cognition and the culture of learning. *Educational Researcher, 18*, 10–12.

Brown, J. S., & Duguid, P. (1991). Organizational learning and communities-of-practice: Toward a unified view of working, learning, and innovation. *Organization Science, 2*(1), 40–57.

Brown, J. S., & Duguid, P. (1993). Stolen knowledge. *Educational Technology, 33*(3), 10–15.

Brown, J. S., & Duguid, P. (1995). Universities in the digital age. *Change: The Journal of the American Academy of Higher Education*. Retrieved June 16, 2008 from http://www.johnseelybrown.com/DigitalU.pdf

Brown, J. S., & Duguid, P. (2000). *The social life of information*. Boston, MA: Harvard Business School Press.

Bryant, A. (2006). *Knowledge management – The ethics of the agora or the mechanisms of the market?* Paper presented at the Proceedings of the 39th Hawaii International Conference on System Sciences.

Cabrera, A., & Cabrera, E. F. (2002). Knowledge-sharing dilemmas. *Organization Studies, 23*(5), 678–710.

Callon, M. (1995). Four models for the dynamics of science. In S. Jasanoff, G. E. Markle, J. C. Petersen, & T. Pinch (Eds.). *Handbook of science and technology studies* (pp. 29–63). Thousand Oaks, CA: Sage.

Chae, B., & Bloodgood, J. M. (2004). *Paradoxes in knowledge management: A dialectical perspective*. Paper presented at the Proceedings of the Tenth Americas Conference on Information Systems, New York.

Ciborra, C. U. (1993). *Teams, markets and systems: Business innovation and information technology*. Cambridge, UK: Cambridge University Press.

Cohen, M. D., & Lee, S. (1991). Editor's introduction. *Organizational science, 2*(1).

Cohen, M. D., & Sproull, L. S. (1996). Introduction. In M. D. Cohen, & L. S. Sproull (Eds.), *Organizational learning*, (pp. ix–xv). Thousand Oaks: Sage.

Cohen, S. G., & Bailey, D. E. (1997). What makes teams work: Group effectiveness research from the shop floor to the executive suite. *Journal of Management, 23* (3), 239–291.

Collins, B., & Margaryan, A. (2004). Applying activity theory to computer supported collaborative learning and work based activities in corporate settings. *Educational Technology Research and Development*, 52(4), 38–52.

Connolly, T., Thorn, B. K., & Heminger, A. (1992). Discretionary databases as social dilemmas. In W. B. G. Liebrand, D. M. Messick, & H. A. M. Wilke (Eds.). *Social dilemmas: Theoretical issues and research findings* (pp. 199–208).Tarrytown: Pergamon Press Inc.

Contu, A., & Willmott, H. (2003). Re-embedding situatedness: The importance of power relations in learning theory. *Organization Science, 14*(3), 283–296.

Cook, S. D. N., & Yanow, D. (1996). Culture and organizational learning. In M. D. Cohen, & L. S. Sproull (Eds.), *Organizational learning* (pp. 430–549). Thousand Oaks, CA: Sage.

Cooney, D. H. (1998). Sharing aspects within *Aspects*: Real-time collaboration in the high school English classroom. In C. J. Bonk & K. S. King (Eds.), *Electronic collaborators: Learner-centered technologies for literacy, apprenticeship, and discourse* (pp. 263–287). Mahwah, NJ: Lawrence Erlbaum Associates.

Cox, A. (2005). What are communities of practice? A comparative review of four seminal works. *Journal of Information Science, 31*(6), 527–540.

Cyert, R. M., & March, J. G. (1963). *A behavioral theory of the firm*. Englewood Cliffs, NJ: Prentice Hall.

Dash, E. (2005, August 7). Europe zips lips; U.S. sells zips. *New York Times*. Retrieved April 30, 2006 from http://www.nytimes.com/2005/08/07/weekinreview/07dash.html?ei=5088&en=e502461cad24f6fe&ex=1281067200&adxnnl=1&partner=rssnyt&emc=rss&adxnnlx=1146430858-8LARDiYu5ae5dJqsu8W3ew

Davenport, E. (2001). Knowledge management issues for online organisations: 'communities of practice' as an exploratory framework. *Journal of Documentation, 57*(1), 61–75.

Davenport, E., & Hall, H. (2002). Organizational knowledge and communities of practice. *Annual Review of Information Science & Technology, 36*(1), 170–227.

Davenport, T. H., Jarvenpaa, S. L., & Beers, M. C. (1996). Improving knowledge work processes. *Sloan Management Review*, 53–65.

Davenport, T. H., & Prusak, L. (1998). *Working knowledge: How organizations management what they know*. Harvard Business School Press.

Davis, F. D. (1993). User acceptance of information technology: system characteristics, user perceptions and behavioral impacts. *International Journal of Man-Machine Studies, 38*(3), 475–487.

DeSanctis, G., & Poole, M. S. (1997). Transition in teamwork in new organizational forms. *Advances in Group Processes, 14*, 157–176.

Desouza, K. C. (2003). Strategic contributions of game rooms to knowledge management: Some preliminary insights. *Information & Management 41*(1), 63–74.

Donner, R. (Director). (1998). Lethal Weapon 4 [Motion picture]. United States: Warner Bros.

Dubé, L., Bourhis, A., & Jacob, R. (2003). *Towards a typology of online communities of practice*. Retrieved on November 11, 2005 from http://gresi.hec.ca/cahier.asp.

Dubé, L., Bourhis, A., Jacob, R. (2006). Towards a typology of virtual communities of practice. Interdisciplinary Journal of Information, Knowledge, and Management, 1, 69–93.

Easterby-Smith, M., Antonacopoulou, E., Simm, D., & Lyles, M. (2004). Constructing contributions to organizational learning: Argyris and the next generation. *Management Learning, 35*(4), 371–380.

Ekbia, H., & Hara, N. (2005). Incentive structures for knowledge sharing. In D. G. Schwartz (Ed.), *Encyclopedia of Knowledge Management* (pp. 237–243). Hershey, PA: Idea Group Publishing.

Elkjaer, B. (2004). Organizational learning: The 'third way.' *Management Learning, 35*(4), 419–434.

Elliott, M., & Kling, R. (1997). Organizational usability of digital libraries: Case study of legal research in civil and criminal courts. *Journal of the American Society for Information Science, 48*(11), 1023–1035.

Fox, S. (2000). Communities of practice: Foucault and actor-network theory. *Journal of Management Studies, 37*, 853–876.

Freeman, P., & Aspray, W. (1999). *The supply of information technology workers in the United States*. Washington, DC: Computing Research Association.

Galegher, J., Kraut, R. E., & Egido, C. (Eds.). (1990). *Intellectual teamwork: Social and technological foundations of cooperative work*. Hillsdale, NJ: Lawrence Erlbaum.

Geertz, C. (1973). *The interpretation of cultures*. New York, NY: Basic Books, Inc.

George, J. F., Iacono, S., & Kling, R. (1995). Learning in context: Extensively computerized work groups as communities-of-practice. *Accounting, Management and Information Technology, 5*(3/4), 185–115.

Gottschalk, P. (1999). Use of IT for knowledge management in law firms. *The Journal of Information, Law, and Technology, 3*. Retrieved April 12, 2005 from http://www2.warwick.ac.uk/fac/soc/law/elj/jilt/1999_3/gottschalk/

Granger, C. A., Morbey, M. L., Lotherington, H., Owston, R. D., & Wideman, H. H. (2002). Factors contribution to teachers' successful implementation of IT. *Journal of Computer Assisted Learning, 18*, 480–488.

Gray, B. (2004). Informal learning in an online community of practice. *Journal of Distance Education, 19*(1), 20–35.

Gray, J. H., & Tatar, D. (2004). Sociocultural analysis of online professional development: A case study of personal, interpersonal, community, and technical aspects. In S. A. Barab, R. Kling, & J. H. Gray (Eds.), *Designing for virtual communities in the service of learning*. Cambridge: Cambridge University Press.

Hall, H., & Davenport, E. (2002). Organizational knowledge and communities of practice. *Annual Review of Information Science and Technology, 36*, 171–227.

Hara, N. (2000). *Social construction of knowledge in professional communities of practice: Tales in courtrooms*. Unpublished doctoral dissertation. Indiana University, Bloomington.

Hara, N., Bonk, C. J., & Angeli, C. M. (2000). Content analysis of online discussion in an applied educational psychology course. *Instructional Science, 28*, 115–152.

Hara, N., & Hew, K. F. (2006). *A case study of a longstanding online community of practice involving critical care and advanced practice nurses*. Paper presented at the Proceedings of the 39th Hawaii International Conference on Information Systems. Retrieved December 29, 2006 from http://csdl2.computer.org/comp/proceedings/hicss/2006/2507/07/250770147a.p

Hara, N., & Hew, K. F. (2007). Knowledge sharing in an online community of health-care professionals. *Information Technology & People, 20*(3), 235–261.

Hara, N., & Kling, R. (2002). *Communities of practice with and without information technologies*. Paper presented at the Proceedings of the 65th Annual Meetings of the American Society for Information Science and Technology, *39*, 338–349.

Hara, N., & Kling, R. (2006). Professional development & knowledge management via virtual spaces. In J. Weiss, J. Nolan, & P. Trifonas (Eds). *International handbook of virtual learning environments*. The Netherlands: Kluwer Academic Publishers.

Hara, N., & Schwen, T. M. (2006). Communities of practice in workplaces: Learning as a naturally occurring event. *Performance Improvement Quarterly, 19*(2), 93–114.

Hara, N., Shachaf, P., & Stoerger, S. (in preparation). Online communities of practice typology revisited.

Harasim, L. (1987). Teaching and learning online: Issues in computer-mediated graduate courses. *Canadian Journal of Educational Communication, 16*(2), 117–135.

Harasim, L. (1990). Online education: An environment for collaboration and intellectual amplification. In L. M. Harasim (Ed.), *Online education: Perspectives on a new environment* (pp. 39–64). New York, NY: Praeger.

Hayes, N., & Walsham, G. (2001). Participation in groupware-mediated communities of practice: a socio-political analysis of knowledge working. *Information and Organization, 11*, 263–288.

Haythornthwaite, C., & Kazmer, M. (2004) (Eds.). *Learning, culture and community in online education: Research and practice*. NY: Peter Lang.

Heath, S. B. (1981). Questioning at home and at school. In G. Spindler (Ed.), *Doing the ethnography of schooling* (pp. 105–131). Prospect Heights, IL:Waveland.

Hendler, G. Y. (2004). Why evidence-based medicine matters to patients? *Journal of Consumer Health on the Internet, 8*(2), 1–14.

Hendriks, P. (1999). Why share knowledge? The influence of ICT on the motivation for knowledge sharing. *Knowledge and Process Management, 6*(2), 91–100.

Henriksson, K. (2000). When communities of practice came to town: On culture and contradiction in emerging theories of organizational learning. *Institute of Economic research Working Paper Series*. Retrieved December 29, 2006 from http://www.lri.lu.se/pdf/wp/2000–3.pdf

Hew, K. F., & Hara, N. (2007a). Knowledge sharing in online environments: A qualitative case study. *Journal of American Society for Information Science & Technology, 59*(14), 2310–2324.

Hew, K. F., & Hara, N. (2007b). Empirical study of motivators and barriers of teacher online knowledge sharing. *Educational Technology Research and Development, 55*(6), 573–595.

Hildreth, P. M. (2004). *Going virtual: Distributed communities of practice*. Hershey, PA: Idea Group.

Huber, G. P. (1996). Organizational learning: The contributing processes and the literature. In M. D. Cohen, & L. S. Sproull (Eds.), *Organizational learning* (pp.124–162). Thousand Oaks, CA: Sage.

Hung, D., Tan, S. C., Hedberg, J. G., & Koh, T. S. (2005). A framework for fostering a community of practice: Scaffolding learners through an evolving continuum. *British Journal of Educational Technology, 36*(2), 159–176.

Hung, D. W. L., & Chen, D. (2001). Situated cognition, Vygotskian thoughts and learning from the comities of practice perspective: Implications for the design of web-based e-learning. *Education Media International, 38*(1), 3–12.

Hur, J., & Hara, N. (2007). How to foster online teacher communities: Factors affecting sustainable online communities for K-12 teachers. *Journal of Educational Computing Research, 36*(3), 245–268.

Huseman, R. C., & Goodman, J. P. (1999). *Leading with knowledge: The nature of competition in the 21st century*. Thousand Oaks, CA: Sage.

Huysman, M. (April, 2002). *Organizational learning and communities of practice: A social constructivist perspective.* Paper presented at the Third European Conference on Organizational Knowledge, Learning and Capabilities. Athens, Greece. Retrieved January 7, 2003 from http://www.alba.edu.gr/OKLC2002/ATHENS2.pdf

Huysman, M. (2003). *Knowledge sharing in practice.* Retrieved April 22, 2003, from http://www.sapdesignguild.org/editions/edition5/print_km_mh.html

Huysman, M., & Wulf, V. (2005). The role of information technology in building and sustaining the relational base of communities. *The Information Society, 21,* 81–89.

Ingersoll, R. M., & Smith, T. M. (2003). The wrong solution to the teacher shortage. *Educational Leadership, 60*(8), 30–33. Retrieved June 24, 2008 from http://www.gse.upenn.edu/faculty_research/docs/EL_TheWrongSolution_to_theTeacherShortage.pdf

Jarvenpaa, S. L., & Leidner, D. E. (1999). Communication and trust in global virtual teams. *Organization Science, 10*(6), 791–815.

Johnson, C. M. (2001). A survey of current research on online communities of practice. *The Internet and Higher Education, 4*(1), 45–60.

Jones, M. O. (1988). In search of meaning: Using qualitative methods in research and application. In M. O. Jones, M. D. Moore, & R. C. Snyder (Eds.), *Inside organizations: Understanding the human dimension,* (pp. 31–47). Newbury Park, CA: Sage.

Jones, M. O. (1991). Why folklore and organization(s)? *Western Folklore, 50*(1), 29–40.

Josefsson, U. (2005). Coping with illness online: The case of patients' online communities. *The Information Society, 21*(2), 133–141.

Kim, S., & Lee, H. (2005). *Employee knowledge sharing capabilities in public and private organizations: Does organizational context matter?* Paper presented at the Proceedings of the 38th Hawaii International Conference on System Sciences.

Kling, R. (1996). Social relationships in electronic forums: Hangouts, salons, workplaces, and communities. In R. Kling (Ed.), *Computerization and controversy: Value conflicts and social choices,* (2nd ed.). San Diego: Academic Press.

Kling, R. & Courtright, C. (2004). Group behavior and learning in electronic forums: A sociotechnical approach. *Building online communities in the service of learning.* (pp. 91–119). Cambridge, UK: Cambridge University Press.

Kling, R., Rosenbaum, H., & Sawyer, S. (2005). *Understanding and communicating social informatics: A framework for studying and teaching the human contexts of information and communication technologies.* Medford, NJ: Information Today.

Kollock, P. (1992). Persuasive communication: Measures to overcome real-life social dilemmas. In W. B. G. Liebrand, D. M. Messick, & H. A. M. Wilke (Eds.), *Social dilemmas: Theoretical issues and research findings,* pp. 307–318. New York: Pergammon.

Kottke, J. (2004, October 27). Normalized data is for sissies. Retrieved June 19, 2008 from http://www.kottke.org/04/10/normalized-data

Krauss, R. M., & Fussell, S. R. (1990). Mutual knowledge and communicative effectiveness. In J. Galegher, R. E. Kraut, & C. Egido (Eds.), *Intellectual teamwork: Social and technological foundations of cooperative work,* (pp. 111–145). Hillsdale, NJ: Lawrence Erlbaum.

Kuchinke, K. P. (1995). Managing learning for performance. *Human Resource Development Quarterly, 6*(3), 307–316.

Lamb, R., & Kling, R. (2003). Reconceptualizing users as social actors in information systems research. *MIS Quarterly, 27*(2), 197–235.

Latour, B. (1987). *Science in action.* Cambridge, MA: Harvard University Press.

Lave, J. (1988). *Cognition in practice.* Cambridge, MA: Cambridge University Press.

Lave, J., & Wenger, E. (1991). *Situated learning: Legitimate peripheral participation.* Cambridge, MA: Cambridge University Press.

Leitzman, D. F. (1981). *Helping behavior in academic settings: Resolving teaching problems.* Unpublished Ed.D. dissertation, Indiana University, Bloomington.

Lesser, E. L., Storck, J. (2001), Communities of practice and organizational performance, *IBM Systems Journal, 40*(4), 831–841.

Levitt, B., & March, J. G. (1988). Organizational learning. *Annual Review of Sociology, 14*, 319–340.

Little, J. W. (2002). Locating learning in teachers' communities of practice: opening up problems of analysis in records of everyday work. *Teaching and Teacher Education, 18*, 917–946.

Miller, D. (1996). A preliminary typology of organizational learning: Synthesizing the literature. *Journal of management, 22*(3), 485–505.

Money, W., & Turner, A. (2004). *Application of the technology acceptance model to a knowledge management system.* Paper presented at the Proceedings of the 37th Hawaii International Conference on System Science. Retrieved June 16, 2008 from http://csdl2.computer.org/comp/proceedings/hicss/2004/2056/08/205680237b.pdf

Montovani, G. (1996). *New communication environments: From everyday to virtual.* London; Bristol, PA: Taylor & Frincis.

Nardi, B. A., Whittaker, S. & Bradner, E. (2000) Interaction and Outeraction: Instant messaging in action. In *Proceedings of the ACM Conference on Computer-Supported Cooperative Work.* New York, ACM Press, pp. 79–88.

Ngwenyama, O. K., & Lyytinen, K. (1997). Groupware environments as action constitutive resources: A social action framework for analyzing groupware technologies. *Computer Supported Cooperative Work: The Journal of Collaborative Computing, 6*(1), 71–93.

Nonaka, I. (1991). The knowledge-creating company. *Harvard Business Review, 69*(6), 96–104.

Nonaka, I. (1994). A dynamic theory of organizational knowledge creation. *Organization Science, 5*(1), 14–37.

Nonaka, I., & Konno, N. (1998). The concept of "ba": Building a foundation for knowledge creation. *California Management Review, 40*(3), 40–54.

Nonaka, I., & Takeuchi, H. (1995). *The knowledge creating company.* New York: Oxford University Press.

Nonaka, I., & Toyama, R. (2005). The theory of the knowledge creating firm: Subjectivity, objectivity and synthesis. *Industrial and Corporate Change, 14*(3), 419–436.

O'Leary, M., Orlikowski, W., & Yates, J. (2002). Distributed work over the centuries: Trust and control in the Hudson's Bay Company, 1670–1826. In P. J. Hinds, & S. Kiesler (eds.), *Distributed work.* Cambridge, MA: MIT Press.

Olson, G., & Olson, J. (2001). Distance matters. *Human Computer Interaction, 15*, 139–179.

Orlikowski, W. J. (1993). Learning from notes: Organizational issues in groupware implementation. *The Information Society, 9*(3), 237–250.

Orlikowski, W. J. (1996) Evolving with notes: Organizational change around groupware technology, In C. U. Ciborra (Ed.), *Groupware and teamwork* (pp. 23–59). England: Wiley.

Orlikowski, W. J. (2002). Knowing in practice: Enacting collective capability in distributed organizing. *Organization Science, 13*(3), 249–274.

Orr, J. E. (1990). Sharing knowledge, celebrating identity: Community memory in a service culture. In D. S. Middleton, & D. Edwards (Eds.), *Collective remembering: Memory in society,* (pp. 169–189). Beverly Hills, CA: Sage.

Orr, J. E. (1996). *Talking about machines: An ethnography of a modern job.* Ithaca, NY: Cornell University Press.

Østerlund, C., & Carlile, P. (2005). Relations in practice: Sorting through practice theories on knowledge sharing in complex organizations. *The Information Society, 21*, 91–107.

Pan, S. L., & Leidner, D. E. (2003). Budging communities of practice with information technology in pursuit of global knowledge sharing. *Journal of Strategic Information Systems, 12*, 71–88.

Parsons, T. (1939). The professionals and social structure. *Social Forces, 17*(4), 457–467.

Pickering, J. M., & King, J. L. (1995). Hardwiring weak ties: Interorganizational computer-mediated communication, occupational communities, and organizational change. *Organization Science, 6*(4), 479–486.

Plaskoff, J. (2003). Intersubjectivity and community-building: Learning to learn organizationally. In M. Easterby-Smith, M. A. Lyles, & K. E., Weick (Eds.), *The Blackwell handbook of organizational learning and knowledge management.* Malden, MA: Blackwell Publishers.

Prusak, L. (2001). Where did knowledge management come from? *IBM Systems Journal, 40*(4). Retrieved August 19, 2007 from https://www.research.ibm.com/journal/sj/404/prusak.html

Quinn, C. N., Mehan, H., Levin, J. A., Black, S. D. (1983). Real education in non-real time: The use of electronic message system for instruction. *Instructional Science, 11*(4), 313–327.

Reiffenstein, T. (2006). Codification, patents and the geography of knowledge transfer in the electronic musical instrument industry. *The Canadian Geographer, 50*(3), 298–318.

Resnick, L. B., Levine, J. M., & Teasley, S. D. (Eds.). (1991). *Perspectives on socially shared cognition.* Washington, DC: American Psychological Association.

Rival, L. (1996). Formal schooling and the production of modern citizens in the eduadorian amazon. In B. A. Levinson, D. E. Foley, & D. C. Holland (Eds.), *The cultural production of the educated person: Critical ethnographies of schooling and local practice,* (pp. 153–167). Albany, NY: State University of New York.

Roberts, J. (2000). From know-how to show-how? Questioning the role of information and communication technologies in knowledge transfer. *Technology Analysis & Strategic Management, 12*(4), 429–443.

Robertson, M., Swan, J., Newell, S. (1996), The Role of networks in the diffusion of technological innovation. *Journal of Management Studies, 33*, 335–361.

Robey, D., Khoo, H. & Powers, C. (2000). Situated learning in cross-functional online teams. *Technical Communication, 47*(1), 51–56.

Ruhleder, K., Jordan, B., & Elmes, M. B. (1996). *Wiring the "new organizaiton": Integrating collaborative technologies and team-based work.* Paper presented at the Annual Meeting of the Academy of Management.

Sabbagh, D. (2006, January 25). No Tibet or Tiananmen on Google's Chinese site. *Times Online.* Retrieved April 30, 2006 from http://business.timesonline.co.uk/article/0,,13132-2008576,00.html

Sackett, D. L., Straus, S. E., Richardson, W. S., Rosenberg, W., & Haynes, R. B. (2000). *Evidence-based medicine: How to practice and teach EBM* (2nd ed.), Edinburgh: Churchill Livingstone.

Schlager, M., Fusco, J., & Schank, P. (1998). Cornerstones for an on-line community of education professionals. *IEEE Technology and Society, 17* (4), 15–21.

Schlager, M., Fusco, J., & Schank, P. (2002). Evolution of an online education community of practice. In K. A., Renninger, & W. Shumar (Eds.), *Building virtual communities: Learning and change in cyberspace* (pp. 129–157). Cambridge, UK: Cambridge University Press.

Schön, D. A. (1983). *The reflective practitioner: How professionals think in action.* New York: Basic Books.

Schultze, U., & Leidner, D. E. (2002). Studying knowledge management in information systems research: Discourses and theoretical assumptions. *MIS Quarterly, 26*(3), 213–242.

Schwen, T. M., & Hara, N. (2004). Community of practice: A metaphor for online design? In S. Barab, R. Kling, & J. Gray (Eds.). *Building online communities in the service of learning* (pp.154–178). Cambridge, UK: Cambridge University Press.

Scott, J. C. (1998). *Seeing like a state: How certain schemes to improve the human condition have failed.* New Haven, CT: Yale University Press.

Selwyn, N. (2000). Creating a "connected" community?: Teachers' use of an electronic discussion group. *Teachers College Record, 102*(4), 750–778.

Senge, P. (1990). *The fifth discipline: The art and practice of the learning organization.* London: Century Business.

Senge, P. (1993). Transforming the practice of management. *Human Resource Development Quarterly, 4*(1), 5–32.

Sharp, J. (1997). *Community of practice: A review of the literature.* Retrieved June 26, 2006, from http://www.tfriend.com/cop-lit.htm

Simon, H. A. (1996). Bounded rationality and organizational learning. In M. D. Cohen & L. S. Sproull (Eds.), *Organizational learning* (pp. 175–187). Thousand Oaks: Sage.

Singer, D. L. (1982). Professional socialization and adult development in graduate professional education. In B. Menson (Ed.), *New directions for experiential learning: Building on experiences in adult development,* no. 16, (pp. 45–63). San Francisco: Joseey-Bass.

Smart, G. (1998). Mapping conceptual worlds: Using interpretive ethnography to explore knowledge-making in a professional community. *Journal of Business Communication, 35*(1), 111–127.

Smith, M. K. (2003). Communities of practice. *The encyclopedia of informal education.* Retrieved on December 13, 2004 from http://www.infed.org/biblio/communities_of_practice.htm

Sproull, L., & Kiesler, S. (1991). *Connections: New ways of working in the networked organization.* Cambridge, MA: MIT Press.

Stamps, D. (2000). Communities of practice: Learning is social. Training is irrelevant? In E. L. Lesser, M. A. Fontaine, & J. A. Slusher (Eds.), *Knowledge and communities* (pp. 53–64). Boston, MA: Butterworth-Heinemann.

Stewart, T. A. (1996, August, 5). The invisible key to success. *Fortune, 134*(3), 173–176.

Suchman, L. (1996). Supporting articulation work. In R. Kling (Ed.), *Computerization and controversy: Value conflicts and social choices* (2nd ed.) (pp. 407–423). San Diego, CA: Academic Press.

Su, J. Z. X. (1992). Sources of influence in preservice teacher socialization. *Journal of Education for Teaching, 18*(3), 239–258.

Swan, J., Robertson, M., & Newell, S. (2002). The construction of 'communities of practice' in the management of innovation. *Management Learning, 33*(4), 477–496.

ThisNation.com (n.d.). U.S. Supreme Court: GIDEON v. WAINWRIGHT, 372 U.S. 335 (1963). Retrieved June 20, 2008 from http://www.thisnation.com/library/gideon.html

Traweek, S. (1988). *Beamtimes and lifetimes: The world of high energy physicists.* Cambridge, MA: Harvard University Press.

Tsang, E. W. K. (1997). Organizational learning and the learning organization: A dichotomy between descriptive and prescriptive research. *Human Relations, 50*(1), 73–89.

Van Maanen, J., & Barley, S. R. (1984). Occupational Communities: Cultures and Control in Organizations. *Research in Organizational Behavior, 6*, 287–365.

Vaughan, D. (1997). The trickle-down effect: Policy decisions, risky work, and the Challenger tragedy. *California Management Review, 39*(2), 80–102.

Von Krogh, G. (1998), Care in knowledge creation. *California Management Review, 40*(3), 133–153.

Vygotsky, L. S. (1978). *Mind in society: The development of higher psychological processes.* Cambridge, MA: Harvard University Press.

Walsh, J. P., & Bayma, T. (1996). Computer networks and scientific work. *Social Studies of Science, 26*, 661–703.

Wasko, M. M., & Faraj, S. (2000). "It is what one does:" Why people participate and help others in electronic communities of practice. *Journal of Strategic Information Systems, 9*, 155–173.

Wasko, M. M., & Faraj, S. (2005). Why should I share? Examining social capital and knowledge contribution in electronic networks of practice. *MIS Quarterly, 29*(1), 35–57.

Weedman, J. (1999). Conversation and community: The potential of electronic conferences for creating intellectual proximity in distributed learning environments. *Journal of the American Society for Information Science, 50*(10), 907–928.

Weick, K. E., & Westley, F. (1996). Organizational learning: Affirming an oxymoron. In S. R. Clegg, C. Hardy, & W. R. Nord (Eds.), *Handbook of organization studies*, (pp. 440–458). London: Sage.

Wenger, E. (1990). *Toward a theory of cultural transparency: Elements of a discourse of the visible and the invisible.* Unpublished doctoral dissertation. University of California, Irvine.

Wenger, E. (1996). Communities of Practice: The social fabric of a learning organization. *Healthcare Forum Journal, 39*(4), 20–27. Retrieved June 25, 2008 from http://www.ewenger.com/pub/index.htm

Wenger, E. (1998). *Communities of practice: Learning, meaning, and identity.* Cambridge: Cambridge University Press.

Wenger, E. (2001). Supporting communities of practice: A survey of community-oriented technologies. Retrieved June 24, 2006 from http://www.ewenger.com/tech/index.htm

Wenger, E., McDermott, R., & Snyder, W. M. (2002). *Cultivating communities of practice: A guide to managing knowledge*. Boston, MA: Harvard Business School Press.

Wenger, E., & Snyder, W. M. (2000). Communities of practice: The organizational frontier. *Harvard Business Review, 78*(1), 139–145.

Whittaker, S., & Schwarz, H. (1999). Meetings of the Board: The impact of scheduling medium on long term group coordination in software development. *Computer Supported Cooperative Work, 8*(3), 175–205.

Yanow, D. (2000). Seeing organizational learning: A cultural view. *Organization, 7*, 247–268.

Zuboff, S. (1988). In the age of the smart machine: The future of work and power. New York, NY: Basic Books.